PSYCHOLOGICAL INQUIRIES.

THE SECOND PART.

BEING A SERIES OF ESSAYS INTENDED TO ILLUSTRATE
SOME POINTS IN THE

PHYSICAL AND MORAL HISTORY OF MAN.

BY

SIR BENJAMIN C. BRODIE, Bart.
D.C.L. F.R.S.
CORRESPONDING MEMBER OF THE IMPERIAL INSTITUTE OF FRANCE ETC. ETC.

LONDON:
LONGMAN, GREEN, LONGMAN, AND ROBERTS.
1862.

PREFACE.

In offering a Second Part of "Psychological Inquiries" to the notice of the public, I have no expectation that it will be found to include any record of facts which were not already known to many of my readers; nor do I doubt that those who have been in the habit of reflecting on these subjects have arrived at conclusions very similar to those at which I have arrived myself.

I have on the present occasion, as I had formerly, two objects especially in view, one of these being to show that the solution of the complicated problem relating to the condition, character, and capabilities of man is not to be attained by a reference to only one department of knowledge; that for this purpose the observations of the physiologist must be combined with those of the moral philosopher, mutually helping and correcting each other, and that either of these alone would be insufficient.

The other object to which I have alluded is, that I would claim for researches of this kind that they should be regarded not as merely curious speculations, but as being more or less of practical importance to every individual among us, enabling us to understand to how great an extent we may contribute to the improvement of the faculties with which we are endowed, and to our own well-being in life.

If I have preserved the mode of dialogue, it is not merely because it is in conformity with the plan of the former volume, but also because it seems to be well adapted to a subject the knowledge of which is not sufficiently complete nor sufficiently well-defined to admit of it being presented in the same systematic form as that which is the foundation of some other sciences.

CONTENTS.

THE FIRST DIALOGUE.

THE SECOND DIALOGUE.

THE THIRD DIALOGUE.

THE FOURTH DIALOGUE.

THE FIFTH DIALOGUE.

THE SIXTH DIALOGUE.

PSYCHOLOGICAL INQUIRIES.

THE FIRST DIALOGUE.

Introduction.—Rural Occupations.—Natural History.—Advantages to be derived from the Study of the Physical Sciences.—No absolute Connexion between Wisdom and Knowledge.—Views of the Turkish Cadi as to the Value of the former.—The other Side of the Question.—Advantageous Co-operation of the Desire of Reputation with the Love of Knowledge.—Importance of Knowledge as furnishing Materials for the Imagination.—The Diffusion of Knowledge the principal Agent in the Extension of Civilization.—Importance of the Science of Mind, as distinguished from Abstract Metaphysics.—Comparison of the Advantage to be derived from the Study of the Physical with that of Mental Science.—The latter to be distinguished from the Discussion of Metaphysical Subtleties.—Human Inquiries limited not only by the Want of Experience, but by the Imperfection of the Human Faculties.—Vain Attempts of Human Curiosity to penetrate beyond these Limits.—Hypotheses may be useful, if taken for no more than they are worth.—Questions beyond the Reach of the Human Intellect.—Superiority of the Modern Method of pursuing Scientific Investigations, as compared with that of

Ancient Times. — The Love of Knowledge the only sure Foundation for Scientific Research. — Danger to the Progress of Knowledge from the too great Intervention of the Utilitarian Principle.

ANOTHER year had passed over our heads. Crites and I, though fully occupied with the duties of our respective professions, had still found some intervals of leisure, in which our minds reverted to our conversations with Eubulus; and I believe that I may say for him, as well as for myself, that we felt that the few days which we had passed in our friend's retreat had not been, on the whole, unprofitably employed. In our daily pursuits we found much that served to illustrate our former speculations, thus giving to our practical dealings with mankind an additional and a higher interest, by connecting them with the great science of human nature. An invitation from our friend to repeat our visit was very acceptable to us, and we again willingly availed ourselves of the opportunity of exchanging for a time the "*fumum et opes strepitumque Romæ*" for the fresh air and quiet of his residence in the country.

We found Eubulus as we had left him, spending some hours in the day among his books and papers, and at other times attending to the not unimportant duties which he had created for himself among his tenants and labourers; especially endeavouring to improve the condition of the latter, not so much by dispensing charity among them (though in this he was not deficient) as by the judicious exercise of his influence, with a view to promote those habits of prudence and forethought and attention to domestic economy, the want of which in that class of society is one principal cause of the inconveniences to which they are subject.

The ornamental grounds adjoining his mansion were not very extensive, but they were laid out with considerable taste, and contained many rare and interesting specimens of the vegetable creation, collected from various regions of the earth. A splendid aloe which, after a repose of many years, was again loaded with flowers, presented a striking contrast to the dark coniferous trees, which by a skilful cultivation were made to flourish as if they had been still in their native climates; while elsewhere a choice collection of orchidaceous plants and other exotics, under the influence of artificial heat, offered themselves as objects of interest not less to the unlearned visitor than to the scientific botanist. Eubulus did not pretend to have paid any unusual degree of attention to the subject; nevertheless he had studied it sufficiently to be able to afford us much curious information as to the economy of plants and vegetable physiology which we had not previously possessed. "Having," he said, "had my mind always a good deal occupied in other ways, I cannot pretend to have dived very deeply into these matters. Nevertheless, even the little knowledge of natural history which I have been able to obtain has been to me a source of much enjoyment since I entered on my present mode of life. In my daily excursions I am not only gratified by the beauty of the landscape, constantly varied as it is, in a hilly country, by the alternations of light and shade, of gloom and sunshine, and in another way by the harmony of rural sounds, so different from the discords of London streets, but I find an additional source of interest in watching the development of buds and flowers, the growth of trees, the progress of plantations, the habits of birds and insects, and all that activity of animal life by which we are surrounded. I should indeed be sorry if the time were ever to arrive when the study of these things was to supersede those other studies which form, as it were, the staple of what is now considered to be the higher kind of education. I can conceive no better method of training the intellectual powers in early life than the acquiring a knowledge of the ancient languages of Greece and Italy; nor any better method of improving the taste, or furnishing the mind with graceful recollections and ennobling sentiments, than an acquaintance with the great writers of antiquity. But I do not see why these should be the exclusive studies of our schools, nor can I doubt that much good would arise from conjoining with them those other studies which relate to the phenomena of the universe. It is not to be supposed, nor is it reasonable to expect, that every one should be a profound astronomer or chemist or naturalist; but some general knowledge of these sciences cannot fail to be useful to us all individually, besides making us more useful members of society as we advance in life."

CRITES. Admitting the force of all that you have said, yet there are circumstances which might lead me to entertain the opinions which you have expressed less confidently than I should have done otherwise. After all, how very little can the greatest amount of human knowledge on these subjects really be! To us the universe presents itself as an assemblage of heterogeneous phenomena, some of which we can reduce to laws of limited operation, while others stand by themselves, bearing no evident relation to anything besides. We may well suppose that there are in the universe Beings of a superior intelligence, and possessed of a greater range of observation, who, if I may be allowed to use such an expression, are sufficiently behind the scenes to be able to contemplate all the immense variety of material phenomena as the result of one great general law impressed on all matter, and to which the whole universe is subjected. But, with our limited capacities, we are compelled to take humbler views, and to grope our way as well as we can among the changes which are taking place around us, as if the mechanical, chemical, and vital laws by which they are governed, were wholly distinct from each other. Then it may be admitted as a question whether it is a matter of course that the extension of human knowledge really leads to an extension of human happiness. Further it may be remarked that the history of science as well as of literature shows that even those who are engaged in these loftier pursuits are not altogether exempt from the frailties of human nature. There is an avarice of reputation, as there is of money; and the competitors have not always been so liberal to each other as they might have been well expected to be. Is it not also really true that there is no connexion between wisdom and knowledge; that there may be much of either one of them with very little of the other;

and that those who have the smallest amount of knowledge are not unfrequently led by their instinct to reason more accurately than some very learned persons, even than those who have studied logic as a science? Taking all this into my consideration, I am sometimes led almost to sympathize with the sentiments expressed by the Turkish Cadi in his farewell letter to Mr. Layard: "There is no wisdom equal to the belief in God. He created the world. Shall we liken ourselves unto Him, in seeking to penetrate into the mysteries of His creation? Shall we say, 'Behold how that star spinneth round that other star'? Let it go. He from whose hand it came will govern and direct it . . . If thou wilt be happy, say 'There is no God but God.' Do no evil, and then thou wilt fear neither man nor death; for surely thine hour will come."

EUBULUS. It is true that the most profound knowledge which man has been able to obtain must be very limited, compared with that which we may suppose to be within the reach of Beings of greater intelligence and power.

Yet, considering the difficulties which stand in his way, and the imperfect means placed at his disposal, it is to me marvellous that so much should have been really accomplished. Could it have been supposed, *à priori*, that a being who under certain circumstances is presented to us as a rude savage, should under other circumstances have become Aristotle or Newton? With regard to your last observations, they amount to no more than this—which I am afraid that I must admit to be true—that neither knowledge nor philosophy is in all cases sufficient to counteract the effect of human frailty. I must also admit that it is not always a pure love of knowledge that stimulates the labours of the philosopher. However sincere that love may be, I will not say that it never happens, but it certainly rarely happens, that the attainment of reputation is not one object to which he looks as the reward of his labours. How can it be otherwise? The desire of reputation,

"The last infirmity of noble mind,"

is an essential part of human nature; an

instinct implanted in us for a wise purpose, and, however it may be misdirected in some instances, productive on the whole of the greatest benefit to mankind. I fully agree with you in the opinion that there may be much of wisdom with little knowledge, and much knowledge with little wisdom; but surely you will not deny that, as a general rule, the effort to acquire knowledge tends to the improvement of the intellect, by bringing into action some of its higher faculties, which might have remained in abeyance otherwise. It may be that an increase of knowledge does not improve the judgment on the facts which are actually brought before us; but it produces an effect which is nearly equivalent, inasmuch as, by extending our observation to a greater number and variety of facts, it enables us to see further, to have broader views, and thus to arrive at more accurate conclusions. You seem to doubt whether the extension of knowledge adds to human happiness; but is it not true that the causes which tend to the shortening of human life are, with few exceptions, such as produce either bodily pain or moral suffering, and that the average period of life is longer in civilized than in uncivilized communities? Then see how the pursuit of knowledge must necessarily operate on those who devote themselves to it; how it elevates the mind to higher views than those which are entertained by the ignorant and the lazy; how it affords worthy objects of contemplation for leisure hours, and supersedes the inclination for low pleasures and mere sensual enjoyments. While other creatures seem to be wholly occupied with the objects which are actually before them, or impelled to the pursuit of those which are more distant by the force of instinct, Man is essentially an imaginative animal. From the materials which his memory affords him, he creates, he abstracts, he makes new combinations: he strives to look into the mysteries of the past, and to lift up the veil which conceals the future. A large portion of life, even that of the dullest person, is spent in the exercise of the imagination. How much, then, must the character of each individual depend on the circumstance of this faculty being worthily directed! I do not say that there are not other studies which will answer the purpose as well, but it cannot be denied that none will answer it better than that of the physical phenomena of the universe around us. Here, more than anywhere else, we find displayed to us that order, and those unmistakable examples of design and of the adaptation of means to ends, by which we are compelled to recognize the agency of one vast superintending Intelligence, and which constitute the sure foundation of natural theology. Here, too, the field to be explored is of unlimited extent. As we advance, the horizon which seems to bound our view recedes further and further from us. Every fresh discovery is but the beginning of a further progress, so that, the more we know, the more we find that we have yet to learn. In this department of knowledge another great advantage is offered to us, inasmuch as, in the different sections of it, the exercise of different faculties of the mind is required. In some we rely almost wholly on simple observation; in others, observation would accomplish little without the aid of experiment; and in others still, where the phenomena are of a simpler kind, and the laws by which they are regulated more exactly determined, the mathematician is enabled to apply his marvellous science, so as to ascertain facts beyond the limits of human experience, and predict changes in the universe which may not be completed before the race of man has ceased to exist on the earth. Thus every variety of the human intellect may find in these studies its suitable employment. The discursive imagination of one, the aptitude for arrangement and classification possessed by another, and the mathematical genius of a third individual, may alike be turned to a good account; and he, who might be held to be stupid if his attention were limited to one subject, may be enabled to show that he too has his peculiar talents by directing it to another.

ERGATES. However he may have expressed himself, I do not suppose that Crites seriously intended to support the views of the

Turkish Cadi, or that he has really any doubt as to the advantages which we may individually derive from the acquirement of knowledge, both as affording us an agreeable occupation, and as tending to improve the moral as well as the intellectual character. But it does more than this. Observe the effect which the general diffusion of knowledge produces on society at large; how it draws the different classes of it into more free communication with each other; how its tendency is to make the laws more impartial, bring even the most despotic governments under the influence of public opinion, and show them that they have no real security except in the good will of the people. Knowledge goes hand-in-hand with civilization. It is necessary to the giving full effect to the precepts of the Christian faith. It was from the want of it that Galileo was tortured by the Inquisition, that Servetus was burned by Calvin, that the Huguenots were persecuted and slaughtered by Louis XIV., and that in numerous other instances one sect of Christians has conceived it to be their duty to exterminate another. It is a misapplication of the term civilization to apply it to any form of society in which ignorance is the rule and knowledge the exception. If a Being of superior intelligence were to look down from some higher sphere on our doings here on the earth, is it to be supposed that he would regard the Duke of Buckingham, dancing at the French Court, and scattering the pearls with which his dress was ornamented, on the floor, as being really superior to an Australian savage; or that he would see in the foreign Prince, who at a later period exhibited himself at another Court with his boots glittering with diamonds, any better emblem of civilization than in the negro chief, who gratifies his vanity by strutting about in the cast-off uniform of a general officer?

But, reverting to the observations which you have just made, you must excuse me for saying that, although you disclaim the intention to do so, you have given a more prominent place to the physical sciences, as objects of inquiry, than really belongs to them. I do not mean to express a doubt as to their great importance, or as to their answering all the purposes which you attribute to them; but it may be a question whether in these times they do not too exclusively occupy our attention, other inquiries which are not less important being comparatively neglected. I refer more especially to those which relate to the operations of the intellect, the laws of our moral sentiments, — in short, all that belongs to the one individual percipient and thinking Being, which each of us feels himself to be. These subjects, which may all be conveniently included under the name of Psychology, constitute a science quite as real as astronomy, chemistry, or natural history; inferior to none of the physical sciences in interest, and I may add in usefulness. I know of no better exercise than that which these inquiries afford for the mind itself, especially as they tend to improve in us the habit of thought and reflection, as they enable us to form a just estimate of our own powers and of the nature and limits of human knowledge; thus rendering us more competent to pursue other inquiries, however different in their nature, with advantage. Observe that I suppose the study of mental phenomena to be properly conducted, and limited to its proper objects, without being adulterated by those wild speculations in which some have indulged, and which have given the science rather a bad reputation under the name of metaphysics.

EUBULUS. It has always happened that at one period the minds of those who observe and think have been more or less exclusively directed to one particular department of knowledge. This is as it should be; for thus by the united efforts of the many a greater progress is made in a particular science or class of sciences than would have been made otherwise. With the ancient Greeks the study of geometry and of moral philosophy in its various branches predominated, and to such an extent that little progress was made by them in the physical sciences. At the present time the latter have taken the place of more abstract speculations, and we see the result in the marvellous progress which has of late been made in unravelling the mysteries of the external world. Another result, however, is that many, and perhaps the majority among us, are too much disposed to look upon the material universe as if it were all in all, and to ignore or disregard those other inquiries to which you have alluded. I, for one, do not underrate their importance, nor in any way differ from the opinion which you have expressed as to their usefulness. I believe that whoever would form a right estimate of himself and others; whoever would improve his own character; whoever aspires to the high office of ameliorating the condition of society, whether as a statesman, as a religious teacher, as the promoter of education, or in any humbler capacity, can in no other way so well qualify himself for his undertaking, whatever it may be, as by studying the laws which regulate his own mind, displayed as it is in his own perceptions, sentiments, thoughts, and volitions. This is the only true foundation of that great science which, for all practical purposes, is more important than anything besides — the science of Human Nature.

Still I cannot persuade myself that if the study of psychology, or, if you please, the moral sciences, were to prevail to the same extent as that of the physical sciences prevails at present, it would lead to any proportionate result. The latter offer to us a domain which is the same as if it were of infinite extent. Every addition to our knowledge leads to knowledge further still; and if that exercise of the imagination, which constitutes the genius of the scientific discoverer as much as it does that of the poet, be regulated by the true spirit of the Inductive philosophy, even where the hypothesis which has led us on is proved to be erroneous, a substance and reality remains, which shows that it has not been employed in vain. But it is quite different as to those studies which have for their object the phenomena and operations of the mind. Here we depend wholly, or almost wholly, on the means afforded by simple observation. The field which is open to us is of limited extent; and ere long we discover that, whatever our powers of observation may be, we can advance no further. If we look into our own minds, up to a certain point there is as much reality as there can be in any other department of human knowledge. So we may learn a good deal as to the varieties of mind as it exists in other men, and even in the inferior animals, and may obtain some, however dim, glimpses of that great creative Intelligence which we see displayed in the order and design of the world in which we live. But we soon arrive where our knowledge ends, and, if we endeavour to overleap this boundary, we pass at once into a region of mists and shadows, where the greatest Intellects do but grope their way to no good purpose, striving to know the unknowable, and speculating on subjects beyond their reach.

ERGATES. If mental science, under the name of metaphysics, has, as I just now remarked, acquired but an indifferent reputation, it is not because the working of the mind is not as fit a subject of observation as the phenomena of the material world, but because metaphysicians have been too apt to mix up with these inquiries the discussion of other which are beyond our capacities. What is the origin of those simple beliefs on which all our knowledge rests? — of that of the existence of the external world? — of something beyond ourselves? — of our own identity? — of the relations of cause and effect? — of the axioms of mathematics? Are these convictions, and various others which might be enumerated, forced upon us by the constitution of our own minds, or are they all resolvable into our experience; and, if so, wherefore do we believe in our experience? Philosophers have not been wanting in their attempts to answer these questions; but they have answered them in different ways, and their speculations have led to no useful or practical result. The convictions remain the same in all of us, complete and unalterable, explain them as we may. But such discussions, however tempting they may be to human curiosity, form no necessary part of the science of psychology, and only tend to injure its character and usefulness.

The fact is, that we are bound and hemmed

in not only by the want of opportunities of experience, but also by the limited nature of our faculties; and that, in this last respect, the difference between one and another department of knowledge is only in degree. One great advantage of that study of our own minds, which constitutes the foundation of psychology, is that, if properly conducted, it leads us more than anything besides to be humble in our aspirations, and not to arrogate to ourselves powers and capabilities which we do not possess. In natural philosophy, or in physiology, many questions arise which are just as incapable of solution as any of those discussed by metaphysicians. I need not advert to the speculations of Plato in the Timæus, nor to those attributed to Timæus the Locrian in the treatise on the Soul of the world, nor to the dreams of Lucretius. The Vortices of Des Cartes, the Phlogiston of Stahl, nay, even the speculations of Newton himself respecting an all-pervading ether, are all examples of human curiosity striving to pass the bounds of human knowledge. An hypothesis which has been once admitted, and to which men's minds have become habituated, will still continue to be taken for granted, long after the slender foundation on which it originally rested has melted away from under it. The notion of an imponderable material agent, as explaining the phenomena of heat — under the name of caloric — was a mere assumption, the more remarkable as it originated with philosophers who dealt less in hypothesis and more in matter of fact than any of their predecessors in the same department of science; yet it continued to prevail long after Sir Humphry Davy, in his Elements of Chemical Philosophy, had demonstrated its fallacy. The argument of Boscovick, showing that we have no grounds for the belief in the existence of solid impenetrable molecules of matter, is unanswerable; yet that other hypothesis which he substituted for it, of mathematical points (that is, points having no dimensions, surrounded by spheres of repulsion and attraction), is even more difficult to realize than that which it was intended to displace.

The truth is, that when we attempt to enter on inquiries such as these, we find that we have arrived at the end of human knowledge, and that our speculations on such subjects as the ultimate molecules of matter, or the magnetic and electric fluids, are merely methods of bringing things which are beyond our comprehension down to the level of our capacities. They are like the x and y in algebra—with this difference, however, that in the one case, in working out the equation, we obtain the value of the unknown quantity, whereas we can arrive at no result analogous to this in the other.

EUBULUS. Yet such hypotheses answer an useful purpose. They enable us, as it were, to bridge over the space which separates the known from the unknown, and to carry our researches into other regions of facts and realities which would have been otherwise inaccessible. But their usefulness fails if we take them for more than they are worth, and forget that they do not themselves constitute knowledge, although they may be employed as instruments to help us in obtaining it. I need scarcely add that there is nothing more essential to the success of scientific inquiry than that we should not waste our time, nor divert our attention from other objects, by speculating on things of which we neither have, nor can have, any actual experience.

ERGATES. The observations which I made were intended to go further than this. It seems to me that, independently of the question of our having or not having opportunities of experience, there are on every side of us things which the structure of our minds does not enable us to comprehend. Do you believe that, under any circumstances, we should be able to understand why it is that a stone gravitates to the earth, or the earth to the sun; or that the sun itself is influenced by the other heavenly bodies, situated at what is to us an inconceivable, though not an immeasurable, distance from it; or that we should ever advance beyond the simple fact that it is so? The same observation may be applied to magnetic attraction and repulsion, and all other analogous agencies. Take another example. All the knowledge and reasoning which we can apply to the subject would lead us to believe that as there are no limits to space, so there are none to the material universe. Yet, if we would represent such Infinity to ourselves; if we try to conceive that, having the requisite power of locomotion, we might pass through worlds and suns, or matter in other shapes, for ever and ever, without arriving at an end, we find that even the imagination fails, and that we are lost in endeavouring to realize an idea which is beyond the reach of our capacities. Again, we recognize certain necessary truths, as, for example, that the square of the base of a right-angled triangle is equal to the squares of the two other sides. This is plain enough. But if we ask why does the Deity exist? why does anything exist? it is evident that it must be from necessity, and because it could not have been otherwise. But we can go no further. The nature of this other kind of necessity is absolutely and entirely beyond all human comprehension. Thus, as we are restrained in one direction by the want of opportunities of experience, so we are in another by the imperfection of our own faculties; and the first thing necessary for the right acquisition of knowledge is, that we should duly recognize the limits which are thus set to our inquiries, and not be led away from that which is real and substantial by the pursuit of the shadowy and fantastic. Referring to the past history of science, it cannot but occur to us how much greater progress would have been made in all its departments, if the cultivators of it had seen their way more distinctly in this respect.

EUBULUS. It is true that what you have now mentioned is among the principal causes which have retarded the progress of science in former times. But you must admit that not only at the present day, but for the last two or three hundred years, these investigations have been on the whole very differently conducted. The objects which are attainable have been better distinguished from those which are not; it has been well understood that in science, as in everything else, we have really nothing to do except with matters of fact, and with that classification of phenomena from which we deduce what are called the laws of Nature. No one now doubts that an exact knowledge of facts is the only basis on which the structure of science can be erected. The astronomer measures the heavens with as much care as a surveyor measures the divisions of an estate. The chemist weighs the results of his experiments with a balance which is affected by the thousandth part of a grain. The geologist, instead of pouncing at once on a Neptunian or Plutonian hypothesis, investigates the structure of different parts of the earth's crust; studies the character and position of the strata, and examines the fossil remains imbedded in them; and reviews the whole of the facts which he has thus collected, before he ventures to draw any conclusions from them.

Ergates. You may add that even in the more complicated sciences of animal physiology and pathology, the importance of exactness as to facts, however difficult the attainment of it may be, is not less fully appreciated than in those which you have enumerated; and if you were to make yourself acquainted with what goes on in a modern hospital with a well-conducted medical school attached to it, you would find that the mode in which investigation as to disease and the operation of remedies is carried on, is perfectly in accordance with the rules which Lord Bacon has laid down for the improvement of medical science in his treatise on the Advancement of Learning. My apology for interrupting you with this remark is, that I have met with not a few of the uneducated part of what are called the educated classes, who seem to think that medical science, especially in that department of it which relates to internal diseases, is little better than a kind of guess-work, in which if correct opinions are formed, it is rather by accident than by any strict process of observation and reasoning.

EUBULUS. I am glad to receive such a confirmation of the views which I have endeavoured to express. If there be any danger to science in the future, it will be not from any want of precision and caution in the conduct of scientific inquiries, but quite of another kind. To love knowledge for its own sake, to find in the advancement of knowledge "its own exceeding great reward," to be impressed with the conviction that, whatever further insight may be obtained into the phenomena and laws of the vast universe around us, the ultimate, though not the immediate result, must be in some way beneficial to mankind, either by administering to their physical necessities and comforts, or by improving their intellectual and moral character,—these have been the principal inducements which have led the greatest geniuses among us, the master-spirits of the age in which they lived, to devote themselves to philosophical and scientific pursuits; and it is thus that they have earned for themselves the respect and homage of the world. Nor can it be said that it is very different from this at the present time. For, whatever worldly advantages the scientific inquirer may in some rare instances derive ultimately from his pursuits, the prospect of them is so distant, and so uncertain, that it can in no way enter into his calculation, or tend to divert his mind from other and more profitable undertakings. But a change is coming over us. The period has arrived when the discoveries of science, the achievements of former generations, are becoming extensively applied to the purposes of commerce, of manufactures, and the ordinary concerns of life. Then the numerous examples which have presented themselves of late years, of large fortunes rapidly accumulated, have afforded an additional stimulus (where none was wanted) to the natural desire of wealth; while the prevailing study of political economy, with all the great good which it has done, has produced this evil, that it has encouraged the disposition, in a large portion of society, to regard the increase of wealth, and the adding to our stock of luxuries and comforts, as the most important business of life. From this combination of causes it is that too many of the public are led to measure the advantages arising from the pursuit of knowledge by a lower standard than that by which it has been measured hitherto; estimating the value of researches in science by their consequences as affecting the physical well-being of mankind, and regarding those who apply the discoveries of philosophers to some practical purpose as if they were on a level with those with whom the discoveries originated. The danger to which I allude is, that the cultivators of science might themselves be led to participate in these utilitarian views. If it should be so, science must undoubtedly descend from the high station which it at present occupies. Nor can this happen without great injury to the cause of knowledge itself. The mere utilitarian philosopher, having his views limited to some immediate practical result, will be like the alchemists of old, as to whom Lord Bacon has observed that "assuredly the search and stir to make gold brought to light a great number of good and fruitful inventions and experiments, as well for the disclosing of Nature as for the use of man's life;" but who, if they had continued their labours to the end of time, would have been no more cognizant of the laws of Nature than they were in the beginning. Eventually, even as to their gross material interests, society would be a loser. The sailor, pursuing his course over the trackless ocean, would never have had placed at his disposal the means of ascertaining the longitude, if philosophers, without reference to this object, had not studied mathematics and the laws of planetary motion; nor would London and Paris have ever been placed, as they now are, in instantaneous communication with each other, if those who began with the simple fact of the muscles of a frog's leg being made to contract by the contact of certain metals, had not pursued these inquiries until they reached the laws of voltaic electricity, never dreaming of the great invention which was ultimately to arise out of these researches in the shape of the electric telegraph. How many analogous instances might not be adduced, sufficient to satisfy the most thorough-going utilitarian that there are none who really contribute so much to the attainment of the objects which he himself has in view, as those who pursue science for its own sake, without reference to the practical results to which it may lead ultimately!

THE SECOND DIALOGUE.

Importance of Self-Knowledge.—Necessity of Physical Power to great Intellectual Exertion.—The distinctive Character of Man, his Capability of Improvement.—Exercise the principal Source of Improvement of both the Physical and the Mental Faculties.—One Sense supplies the Deficiency of another.—Illustrations of this Rule.—The Influence of Education in placing the other Conditions of the Mind under Subjection to the Will.—Various Illustrations of the Phenomena and Laws of Memory.—Artificial Aids to Memory.—Peculiar Memories.—Connexion of the Imagination with Memory.—Importance of the Imagination.—The Judgment more improved by the Prosecution of the Inductive than by that of the Deductive Sciences.—Perfection of different Faculties in different Individuals, the Excellence of one supplying the Deficiency of another.—Patience, Diligence, and Perseverance.—Influence of Conversation on the Development of the Mental Faculties, but Habits of Reflection best acquired at other Times.

It was on the morning after our last conversation that Crites thus addressed Eubulus:—

"When you took leave of us last year, referring to the duties which we owe to society and ourselves, you observed that 'no one can perform them properly who does not regard his own powers, his own disposition, and his peculiar moral temperament, influenced as it may be by his physical condition and his mode of life, as a fit object of study, as much as anything external to himself.' Now, agreeing with you in this opinion, it appears to me that this is a lesson which cannot be learned too early in life; and that the teaching it is a duty to the performance of which the attention of those to whom the business of education is intrusted should be especially directed."

EUBULUS. I suspect that it would be dangerous to lay down any express rule for young people, that they should look into and study their own characters; and that it would lead at least as often to self-conceit as it would to humility. But a judicious parent or a judicious tutor may accomplish the same object by other means, by availing himself of accidental opportunities of training the mind of his child or pupil in a right direction. In the observations to which you refer, I had in view chiefly those who are so far advanced in life that they may be expected to educate themselves; and it is then, and then only, when the lesson is forced upon us by the rough usage of the world, that it will be effectually learned. I need not repeat what moralists have so often told us, as to the necessity of correcting our propensities to evil and encouraging our propensities to good. But surely it is important that individually we should also do what we can towards the improvement of our intellectual faculties; and these are so bound up with our bodily condition, that we cannot, with any advantage, direct our attention to the one while we disregard the other. Each individual must study his own case. Habits of life in which one may indulge with apparent impunity, may be injurious to the intellect of another. What any of us may be able to accomplish, depends, in a great degree, on the extent of our physical powers. There are many who have attained the highest academic honours, and have been enabled immediately afterwards to enter, with all the energy required, into the active business of life, simply because the attainment of those honours was to them a comparatively easy task. But there are many others who have attained the same object with difficulty, and whose powers had been thereby so far exhausted as to render them incapable of any great undertakings afterwards.

ERGATES. It is a general law of the animal economy, that when the vital powers are from any cause depressed below a certain point, they are not easily, and sometimes are never, repaired. I have known persons who were otherwise healthy suffer from the effect of a large loss of blood for some years afterwards; and there are numerous instances of those who for a limited time have been subjected to great hardships and privations, who have never regained their former condition. In this age of keen competition, there are not a few who suffer from too great mental, as there are others who suffer from too great bodily labour, and who would accomplish greater things in the end if their exertions were more limited. In the way of illustration, I might, if I were so disposed, refer to instances both of professional men and of politicians who apparently from this cause have broken down in the middle of what appeared to be a noble and prosperous career. Much more might be said on the subject; but after all there is one simple rule, the observation of which is in itself sufficient: to make the most of the intellectual powers, the animal system should be maintained in a state approaching as nearly as possible to that of perfect health; and all those habits, whatever they may be, which tend in any degree to derange the animal functions, should be scrupulously avoided.

EUBULUS. There is, however, no necessary connexion between robust health and superior intelligence. How often do we see the former combined with stupidity and ignorance! Travellers report to us instances of tribes of savages who intellectually appear not to be many degrees superior to the lower animals. The same may be said of the poor deserted children who have been sometimes found leading a lonely life and maintaining a precarious existence in forests, apart from all human society. In his rude and uncultivated state, there is little in man either to respect or admire. That by which he is distinguished, and which elevates him above all other creatures on earth, is his capability of improvement. The observation applies to individuals not less than it does to societies of men. Of two individuals, with perhaps equal capacities of mind, but placed under different circumstances as to education and as to the class of persons with whom they associate in early life, one may be found, after a lapse of years, to be comparatively stupid, while the other, as to intelligence, far surpasses what had been anticipated of him in the beginning.

Crites. But here the question arises, "Are all our faculties alike capable of improvement? and if it be so, is the same method of treatment which is applicable to one of them applicable to all the rest?"

Eubulus. For all practical purposes it may be sufficient to lay it down as a rule that the faculties of the mind generally, like those of the body, are strengthened by exercise. To give an explicit answer to your question, however, we must consider the subject more in detail; and probably the prudent course will be to begin where our knowledge begins, that is, with the organs of sense. But, instead of entering upon it myself, I would rather refer you to Ergates, whose opinion on this, as on many other subjects, is more valuable than mine.

ERGATES. I really have little more to say respecting it than may have occurred to any one else. It may indeed be almost resolved into this simple rule: that our senses admit of being improved by cultivation as much as those higher faculties to which they are subservient. The sailor distinguishes a ship in the horizon which is imperceptible to the landsman. The practised musician has a nicer perception of musical sounds, of harmonies and discords, than the inexperienced artist. The painter who has become a master of his art recognizes effects of shades and colours, and a multitude of things besides, of which he took no cognizance at all when he first entered on his profession as a student. So also the water-drinking Hindoo finds a difference of taste in the waters of different springs, which are alike insipid to the drinkers of beer or wine; and the worker in jewelry and gold ornaments acquires a nicety of touch of which the blacksmith can form no conception. It is, however, in those cases in which a particular sense has never existed, or has been permanently destroyed, that we learn to how great an extent other senses may be improved so as to supply the deficiency. In the earlier part of my life I made acquaintance with a blind fiddler, who wandered about the country by himself, attending village festivals; and I remember, among many other things which I have now forgotten, his having described to me how certain feelings, produced, as he supposed them to be, by the pressure of the air, made him understand that he was close to a large tree. Children who have been born blind, or who have become blind, learn to read with their fingers, by means of small embossed characters, in a shorter space of time than those who have their sight do by printed books. They become as familiar with the voices of their acquaintance as others are with their countenances; and it is really true that they not unfrequently wonder why, from being born blind, they should be held to be objects of commiseration.

I remember seeing a little girl three or four years old, who had been totally deaf from the time of her birth, watching her mother as she was speaking. The intensely earnest and anxious expression of her countenance when she was thus occupied was almost painful to behold; but the result was, that by a close attention to the motions of the lips, and, as I presume, by observing those smaller movements of the features which are unnoticed by others, she was enabled to obtain a competent knowledge, not indeed of what her mother said, but of what she meant to say. Examples of this kind may be supplied without end. There are few professions, and few pursuits in life, which do not require that some one organ of sense should be in a state of greater perfection than the rest; and each individual accordingly trains and educates that of which he is most in need, though he himself is unconscious that he is doing so.

The organs of sense are as much physical machines as the telescope, or the microscope, or the ear-trumpet ; and in like manner, as the muscles become more developed, more vascular, and larger by being exercised, so it is not improbable some such actual changes take place in the organs of sense also, rendering them more adapted to the purposes for which they are designed. But this does not explain the whole. Any one who enters on the study of minute anatomy, or what they are pleased to call *histology* (we are very fond in these times of inventing new names for old things), by means of the microscope, is at first very awkward in the use of the instrument. By degrees he understands it better, and is enabled to see what he could not see, or at any rate did not comprehend, in the beginning. So it is with regard to the organs of sense. We are clumsy in applying them to a new purpose, as we may be clumsy in our first attempts with an optical machine, but by diligence and attention we become more dexterous. What I am about to mention is no rare occurrence, and will serve to explain what I believe to be the correct view of the subject. A gentleman, who heard perfectly well with one ear, was thoroughly convinced that he had been entirely deaf with the other ear from the time of his being a child. Bye-and-bye he became affected with a severe inflammation of the sound ear, and, when this had subsided, he discovered to his dismay that he had become quite deaf on this side also. After some time, however, on his being compelled to make a trial of what he called his deaf ear, he found that it was not really so useless as he had supposed it to be. By constant attention to the neglected organ, his capability of hearing with it gradually increased, and to such an extent that, with the help of an ear-trumpet, he could hear sufficiently well for the purposes of conversation.

CRITES. Still you seem to be of the opinion that the more constant and more exact use of the ear, or the eye, or of the organ of touch, may ultimately lead to some actual physical change in their condition; and it being so, I do not see that you can well avoid the conclusion, that the greater development of any one of the mental faculties may be attended with some corresponding change in the organization of those parts of the brain which are subservient to it.

ERGATES. Indeed, I admitted what amounts to nearly the same thing when we were discussing the subject of the generation of new instincts last year. But what these changes are we have no means of knowing, neither can we form the smallest conception of them, so that our only safe way is to disregard them altogether. To extend the inquiry in this direction, or otherwise than as a branch of intellectual or moral philosophy, would be a hopeless undertaking.

I have told you what occurs to me as to the mode in which we learn to make a better use of the organs of sense. But I am aware that this goes very little way towards explaining the process of improvement as to the higher faculties. What is the nature of that process? Is it the same in all cases? or is one faculty to be improved in one way, and another in another way?

EUBULUS. Excuse me if I interrupt you by offering an observation in illustration of the questions which you have just proposed. In the account of one of Captain Cook's voyages of discovery in the Pacific Ocean, it is stated that nothing was more remarkable in the untutored islanders of that region than the rapidity with which they passed from one state of even violent emotion to another, as from joy to grief, or from anger to kindness. The fact is, that those states of mind which constitute the emotions and passions are all capable of being influenced by the will. We may give way to them, we may contend against them, we may by an effort of the will prolong or shorten their duration; and accordingly as we habituate ourselves to make the necessary effort, so does our dominion over them become more complete. This is the first moral duty which a good education imposes on us in childhood. It is the lesson taught us by the sermon on the Mount, and by the best heathen moralists. It is the basis on which civilization rests; and if the highest civilization in this respect falls far short of our ideal standard of what it ought to be, it is not because the principle is erroneous, but because man is imperfect. Now that which is true as to those mental conditions to which I have just adverted, is also true as to some of those which we class under the head of "intellectual faculties." The objects presented by the imagination are not summoned before us by any voluntary effort. Their presence, their absence, the order in which they appear, are independent of any direct influence which we have over them. Nevertheless, when they are brought before us, we can arrest them in their progress; we can look at them on every side, so that all their various relations shall be gradually presented to our view; and we can dismiss them when we please. All this is done by an effort of the will; and in proportion as we accustom ourselves to make it, so does that effort become more easy, and our dominion over the imagination more complete.

The power of continued attention differs very much in different individuals, according to the original construction of their respective minds. Thus in the case of two boys, apparently under similar circumstances, we may find one of them to have great difficulty in fixing his attention long enough to enable him to understand the simplest proposition in geometry, while the other accomplishes the same thing with no difficulty at all. But here also the defect under which the one labours may be in a great degree supplied by education and practice, while the advantage which the other naturally possesses may be lost by neglect. A young man who has not been trained to gain knowledge by reading, will complain that, after he has read a few pages, his mind becomes bewildered, and he can read no longer; and I have known even those who have been well educated originally to make the same complaint, when, from being constantly engaged in the active pursuits of life, they have for many years neglected the habit of reading. On the other hand, the boy who is supposed to have *no head for mathematics* may by constant practice become a competent mathematician. It is the same in this case as in that of the imagination. The mind is kept fixed on one object, or succession of objects, by an effort of the will; and the more we are habituated to make the effort, the more easy it becomes to make it.

CRITES. Of course it is the same as to our other mental faculties — the memory for example. A bad memory may be strengthened by exercise, and the best memory may be impaired by neglect.

EUBULUS. I do not know that this is a matter of course, though I admit that what you say is true to a certain extent. As Dr. Hooke has observed, to remember anything an effort of attention is required; and as the habit of attention may be improved by exercise, so may the memory also. But it is only an indirect influence that the will possesses over this wondrous faculty. Observe what happens with regard to an individual act of memory. We cannot remember an event, or anything else, simply by willing to do so; for to know what we wish to remember is, in fact, to remember it already. Take a particular example. You desire to recollect the author of a poem: you keep the subject before your mind until, by what is called the association of ideas or suggestion, some circumstances connected with it present themselves to you, such as the book in which you formerly read the poem in question, the place in which you were at the time, or the individual who quoted it, until at last the name of the author flashes suddenly upon you. Perhaps this may not happen until a long time afterwards, and when you least expect it. On some occasion formerly, two Latin lines recurred to my memory, of which I tried in vain to recollect the writer, or where I had seen them. I searched for them in various authors, and made inquiries of some of my friends, but without success. It was not until after the lapse of some five or six years that some accidental circumstance all at once reminded me that they were in a manuscript prize poem which had been lent to me to read, and which I had had in my possession only for a single evening, at least twenty years ago. Instances similar to this must be familiar to all of us.

It has happened to me (and I dare say that the same thing has happened to you) to have circumstances which had occurred when I was a boy, and which it might be supposed that I had entirely forgotten, present themselves to me again in a dream. The vagaries of our memory during sleep are indeed very remarkable: it seems to deal with things and events that have long since passed away, much more than it does with those which have occurred lately; and this is more especially the case as we advance in life.

ERGATES. What you have now mentioned may probably be explained by the well-known fact that the impressions made on the mind in early life are stronger and more lasting than those which are made afterwards. But there are other things connected with the memory which are not to be explained so easily. Take this for example. It has often occurred to myself, and I know that it has to others also, when some new event has taken place, to have a strong impression that the same thing has happened before, although I know that it is not and cannot be so in reality. If I am not mistaken, it was held by Plato that this is neither more nor less than some partial reminiscence of a former life.

EUBULUS. It seems to me that the circumstance to which you have alluded admits of a much more reasonable solution than that offered by the Athenian philosopher. Is it not the case that on these occasions there is always an actual revival of some impression made on the mind formerly, though the events in connexion with it have escaped from our memory? You will, I am sure, not think that I make too great a demand on your attention if I read to you an extract from a letter which I have received from a very intelligent correspondent, which throws great light on the subject, and which seems fully to confirm the opinion which I have ventured to express:—

"When I was about fifteen years of age I went, with my father and mother and other friends, on a tour through Somersetshire; and having arrived at Wellington, where I had certainly never been before, we tarried an hour or two at the 'Squirrel' Inn for refreshments. On entering the room where the rest of the party were assembled, I found myself suddenly surprised and pursued by a pack of strange, shadowy, infantile images, too vague to be called recollections, too distinct and persevering to be dismissed as phantasms. Whichever way I turned my eyes, faint and imperfect pictures of persons once familiar to my childhood, and feeble outlines of events long passed away, came crowding around me and vanishing again in rapid and fitful succession. A wild reverie of early childhood, half illusion, half reality, seized me, for which I could not possibly account; and when I attempted to fix and examine any one of the images, it fled like a phantom from my grasp, and was immediately succeeded by another equally confused and volatile. I felt assured that all this was not a mere trick of the imagination. It seemed to me rather that enfeebled memory was, by some sudden impulse, set actively at work, endeavouring to recall the forms of past realities, long overlaid and almost lost behind the throng of subsequent events. My uneasiness was noticed by my mother; and when I had described my sensations, the whole mystery was speedily solved by the discovery that the pattern of the wall-paper in the room where we were seated was exactly similar to that of my nursery at Paddington, which I had never seen since I was between four and five years of age. I did not immediately remember the paper, but I was soon satisfied that it was indeed the medium of association through which all those ill-defined, half-faded forms had travelled up to light; my nurse and nursery events associated with that paper pattern being, after all, but very faintly pictured on the field of my remembrance."*

CRITES. I do not complain of this digres-

* For this interesting communication, the author is indebted to the kindness of the Reverend Thomas Bacon, Rector of Kingsworthy, Hants.

sion, which relates to a question which has often excited my curiosity. But you must excuse me if I revert to a former part of our conversation, the subject of which is far from being exhausted.

If the memory cannot be improved in one way, it may be in another. I refer especially to the various methods which have been proposed of artificial memory, and to some of which I myself frequently have recourse with advantage.

EUBULUS. It is not very correct to say that these methods improve the memory. The more proper expression would be that they help it on special occasions, which is quite a different thing.

> "Thirty days hath September,
> April, June, and November,
> February has twenty-eight alone,
> And all the rest have thirty-one;
> But leap-year, coming once in four,
> Gives to February one day more."

Here the rhythm of six lines enables us to recall to our minds thirteen facts, which, having no connexion with any general rule, we might not easily remember otherwise. In the same manner the *memoria technica* of Gray enables us not to remember but to find out dates when we want them. Dr. Wallis *, who nearly two centuries ago was professor of geometry at Oxford, attained the power of making arithmetical calculations, " without the assistance of pen and ink, or aught equivalent thereunto," to such an extent, that he extracted the square root of three down to twenty places of decimals. We must indeed suppose him to have had originally some peculiar aptitude for such calculations; but he describes himself to have acquired it by practising at night and in the dark, when there was nothing to be seen, and nothing to be heard, that could disturb his attention. Dr. Wallis's communication to the Royal Society on this subject contains much curious information; and it is well worth your while to refer to it, when you have the opportunity of doing so.

* Philosophical Transactions, vol. xv. p. 1269.

Some years ago an ingenious person, who called himself the "Professor Von Feinagle," delivered some lectures at the Royal Institution on a system of artificial memory which he had invented, and which seems in some instances to have led to some very remarkable results. The process was too complicated for me to trouble you with an account of it; it was moreover too laborious to be practically useful, and it is no matter of wonder that it should be now forgotten. The fact is (as I said before) that such artificial contrivances as this was, do not really improve the memory, any more than the telescope which enables us to see distant objects improves the sight, or an ear-trumpet improves the sense of hearing.

ERGATES. In the course of our conversations last year, I mentioned several facts which seem to show that there is some kind of connexion between the function of memory and the organization of the brain; and it is easy to suppose that as in some persons there is a more delicate structure of the nerves of hearing, enabling them to have a nicer perception of musical sounds than is possessed by others, so there may be a difference in the organization of that part of the brain which is in some way or other subservient to the memory, accounting for the great difference as to the degree of perfection in which we find this faculty to exist in different individuals.

EUBULUS. However that may be, and admitting that the memory may be improved by use and damaged by neglect, it is plain that there is a vast original difference in the power of memory in different persons. A Spanish theologian, Francis Suarez, is reported to have been able to repeat the whole of the voluminous works of St. Augustine by heart; while Montaigne speaks of his own memory as being so bad that he ought to be celebrated for its imperfection — at the same time consoling himself with the reflection that therefore he never could venture to tell lies. Then there are different kinds of memory. One person has no memory for names or other insulated facts, while he remembers with the greatest ease whatever can be referred to a general rule; in another it is just the reverse. Jedediah Buxton had a vast memory for figures; another finds it difficult to cast up even a few figures in a simple lesson in arithmetic. It may be said that all these differences may be resolved into the different degree of attention which, according to our respective inclinations and tastes, we bestow on different subjects. But this is not all; for you will repeatedly see one person who remembers things with what may be regarded as a moderate effort of attention, while another fails though he take the greatest pains to do so.

CRITES. I know that Montaigne complains on more than one occasion of his want of memory, and indeed, according to his own account of himself, it must in some respects have been bad enough. He says, "I must have three hours to learn three verses;" and again, "If any one would propose anything to me, he must do it by parcels, for to answer a speech consisting of several heads I am not able." But the truth is, that his must have been an instance, similar to those which you have mentioned, of a person having a memory for one thing and not for another. The multitude of apposite quotations which he has made from books, and the variety of facts referred to in his essays, show that he possessed one kind of memory at least in great perfection, however much he may have been deficient in other kinds.

Do you believe that any one can accomplish any great things in this world, whether it be in general literature, in science, in politics, or in the ordinary affairs of life, whose memory is defective?

EUBULUS. There can be but one answer to your question. In proportion as the memory is defective, so do we lose the advantage which we should otherwise derive from our experience of the past, of that knowledge by which alone we are enabled to anticipate the future. With an imperfect memory there must be but a scanty imagination, the images presented by the latter being altogether supplied from the stores already accumulated in the mind. The materials are the same, the only difference being, that in the two cases they are differently combined. I need not expatiate on the important place which the imagination occupies in all our intellectual operations; it may, indeed, well be regarded as the most important, as it is probably almost the peculiar, attribute of man. We are indebted to it for the greatest discoveries in science, the greatest improvements in the arts; without it, no one can arrive at excellence as a statesman, or as the commander of armies, any more than as a poet or the writer of romances. Observe that I speak of a well-regulated imagination, which is kept in subjection to the judgment; and not that wild imagination which is allowed to wander without control, and which leads to nothing but folly and mischief.

Returning to the subject of memory, I may observe that as there are different kinds of memory, so these are of very different degrees of value. Jedediah Buxton's memory of figures ended where it began. Dr. Wallis would have been just as great a mathematician if he had never performed those arithmetical exploits which I just now mentioned. He could have accomplished the same thing quite as well with a pencil and paper, and with a less expenditure of nervous force. If it be really true that the Spanish theologian knew all St. Augustine's works by heart, it does not appear that this was ever productive of any real good either to himself or to any one else. I did not myself know the individual; but I have been informed, on what I believe to be very good authority, of an instance of a young man who, after once or twice reading it, could repeat a rather long ballad, and yet, when he had done so, did not know the meaning of it. The memory which really leads to great results is that which is founded not on mere juxtaposition, but on the relations which objects and events have to each other: one suggesting another, so that they present themselves not as insulated facts, but as parts of a whole. It is this kind of memory which distinguishes the philosophical historian from the dry narrator of wars, and treaties, and party politics; which opens to the view of the scientific inquirer those resemblances and analogies by means of which he is enabled, in the midst of apparent confusion and complexity, to trace simplicity and order, and to arrive at a knowledge of the general laws which govern the phenomena of the universe; and which leads those whose genius takes another course "to find in poetry its own exceeding great reward," or "to look for the good and the beautiful in everything around them;" at the same time that they become the benefactors of mankind, by transmitting wise thoughts and noble sentiments to the generations which come after them.

CRITES. You may add — or rather the fact is included in what you have just now stated — that it is this kind of memory which affords the greatest help to the reasoning powers and the judgment, by giving us a broader view of the thing before us, and thus qualifying us for a more efficient exercise of these intellectual processes. But is not this in contradiction to the opinion which you expressed formerly, that the undisciplined mind reasons and judges not less accurately than that which has been the most highly cultivated?

EUBULUS. It is not at all so if it be true, and I cannot doubt it being so, that the kind of memory which each of us possesses is a natural gift, and admitting of being influenced only to a very limited extent by any special education or training. I said that there might be little knowledge with much wisdom, and little wisdom with much knowledge, and that a child or a peasant may reason as accurately on the facts which he actually knows and comprehends, as those who have made it their business to study logic as a science; and I say so still. In the Exact sciences there is only one side to each question, and those who comprehend the data are inevitably led to one and the same conclusion, while those who do not comprehend them arrive at no conclusion at all. In the Inductive sciences, and in the ordinary affairs of life, the case is different. Here our judgment is to be founded on a comparison of the evidence on one side with the evidence on the other; and some minds are so constructed that they do this readily and at once, while other minds, having a more limited range, do so with difficulty or not at all, so that they seem to be scarcely capable of seeing both sides of a question. The investigation of the laws of reasoning is an important branch of philosophy; but in practice you will find that the ablest reasoners are those who follow their instinct, without reference to any of the rules laid down by logicians. The advantage afforded by a larger amount of knowledge on any given subject, is, not that it enables you to reason better, but that it gives you more sufficient data for the purpose. At the same time I admit that in this, as in other matters, the effect of practice is to make us more perfect. In other words, we may profit by experience, and learn, from every blunder which we make by drawing our conclusions too hastily, to be more circumspect and cautious afterwards.

The intellectual not less than the moral character of individuals is formed by a variety of circumstances. In some one faculty, in others another faculty, exists in greater perfection than the rest; and as, on the one hand, any one of them may run to waste if neglected, so, on the other hand, it may be improved by exercise, especially during the early period of life. Much depends on early education, on the knowledge and the kind of knowledge which we have acquired, on the society in which we live, on our habits and worldly pursuits. One man may be stimulated by necessity, another by ambition, to make the most of the faculties, whatever they may be, which God has given him; another may have no such inducement to exertion; and hence it often happens that he of whom in early life a great deal is expected, is soon left behind in the race by another, of whom there had been no such sanguine anticipations.

You can form no real measure of the intellect by what appears on the surface. The most fluent speaker may be good for nothing else. Neither can you do so by observing the perfection or imperfection of a single faculty, for the excellence of one may compensate the deficiency of another. One man may have a greater capacity for long-continued attention, and for the acquirement of knowledge; another, who is his inferior in this respect, may nevertheless have the advantage over him by being endowed with a more keen and rapid perception and a greater capability of independent thought. We see those who devote themselves to books, and remember all that they have read, and others who have little disposition, and even find it difficult, to acquire knowledge in this manner, but who obtain the same result by observing and studying things themselves. The latter may indeed have a smaller amount of information, but they have a more real and substantial, and a more enduring knowledge. The intellectual powers may be above the average, and yet be exercised to little purpose, because the possessor of them, either from a want of self-knowledge or from the force of circumstances, is not in the place for which he is qualified. What would Cromwell have been if he had remained a brewer? or Moreau, if the revolutionary convulsion had not raised him from being a small attorney to be the commander of armies?

CRITES. You say nothing of the minor qualities of patience, diligence, and perseverance, which nevertheless play no unimportant part in all human pursuits.

EUBULUS. Do not call these the minor qualities; it seems to me that there are none really more important. They rarely exist except in combination with the higher order of intellect. Great things are accomplished only by those who, confident in their own powers, view the far-distant object with a strong determination to attain it, and persevere in their efforts in spite of difficulties and disappointments.

> "Pater ipse colendi
> Haud facilem esse viam voluit; primusque per artem
> Movit agros, curis acuens mortalia corda."

The application of this rule is not limited to agriculture. Let no one persuade himself into the belief that he is to be carried forward by what he may be pleased to call "the force of genius." The most retentive memory, the quickest perception, nay, even the soundest judgment, will of themselves lead to no grand results. For these not only is labour required, but it must be persevering labour, not diverted from one object to another by caprice or the love of novelty, but steadily pursuing its course amid failures and disappointments. In fact, if there be anything which deserves the name of genius, those which you have rather incautiously designated as minor qualities are an essential part of it. Without them there would have been no advancement in Science, no improvement in Art; or, to express what I mean to say in a few words, there would have been nothing of what constitutes the higher form of civilization.

There is one other quality not less essential than those of which I have just been speaking. For this I can find no other English name than that of humility; though that does not exactly express my meaning. It is that quality which leads a man to look into himself, to find out his own deficiencies and endeavour to correct them, to doubt his own observations until they are carefully verified, to doubt also his own conclusions until he has looked at them on every side, and considered all that has been urged, or that might be urged, in opposition to them. It is such habits as these which lead to the highest distinction, for they lead to a knowledge of the truth and to self-improvement. There is no other foundation for a just self-confidence. In this sense of the word the greatest men are humble. They may be proud — they are sometimes even vain; but they are never conceited. Self-conceit belongs to the smaller intellects,—to those who, having in reality some dim perception of their own incapacity, derive consolation from comparing themselves, not with their superiors, nor even with their equals, but with those who are their own inferiors.

Although I fear that you are already wearied by my thus propounding to you my own notions, and that you may with good reason be ready to say "We knew all this before," yet I am tempted to tax your patience for a few moments more. There is a passage which occurs somewhere in the writings of Miss Martineau, though I cannot tell you exactly where to find it, which deserves the attention of those who wish to make the best use of their intellect. I do not remember the precise words, but they are to this effect, that it is important that whoever is engaged in the active pursuits of life should have a certain portion of the day in which he may be alone, in order that he may have the opportunity of communing in private with himself. In conversation with others our perceptions are rendered more acute; the mind works more rapidly; new views of things, even of those with which we are most familiar, present themselves as if it were by magic. They may be right or wrong, but they satisfy us at the time, as they help us in our argument. All this is good in its way, and we know that those whose minds have not been accustomed to be brought into collision with the minds of others are apt to become stupid, and (as in the case of long-continued solitary confinement) even idiotic. But, to turn what we gain from conversation to the best account, we require that there should be intervals in which our ideas may flow uninterruptedly, without being diverted in their course by the remarks of others. It is in such intervals that we best learn to think. I know not what may be the experience of others, but I acknowledge that in these ways I have not unfrequently derived an ample compensation for the wearisome hours of a sleepless night. Not only are hours of relaxation truly as necessary a part of education as hours of study, but I will go further than this, convinced as I am that, if we could unravel the whole chain of causes and effects, we should find that it has often happened that, in the solitary rambles of a pensive boy, the foundation has been laid of noble thoughts and great undertakings in the after-periods of his life. It is stated in the life of Sir Walter Scott that it was while he was a sickly boy, residing for the benefit of his health in a farm-house, some of those visions passed before his mind which in the after-part of his life assumed a more substantial form, and delighted the world in the pages of "Waverley" and "Old Mortality."

THE THIRD DIALOGUE.

Influence of External Circumstances on the Condition of the Mind.—To be counteracted in a great Degree by Voluntary Effort.—Exercise of the Intellect necessary to its Healthy Condition, and conducive to Happiness and Bodily Health.—Formation of Individual Character.—Free-will and Necessity.—Baron Alderson.—Nervous Force expended in one Way cannot be expended in another.—Emotions and Passions.—The Intellect and Emotions Necessary Parts of the same System.—State of Mind very much dependent on that of the Circulating Blood.—This Rule variously illustrated.—Man being a Gregarious Animal, his Relations to others cannot be overlooked.—Cheerfulness of the Mind dependent on the Animal Functions being properly performed.—However important the Mental Faculties may be in one Way, the Corporeal Faculties are not less important in another.—Dangers to Society if the latter were to be deteriorated.

It was a bright morning in the early part of August. A thunderstorm on the preceding evening had cooled the atmosphere, refreshed the plants in the flower-beds, and moistened the earth which had been parched by the previous heat. The sun, still far below the meridian, with a few light clouds occasionally passing over it, rendered the air of an agreeable temperature. After breakfast we had strolled into the garden, and for some time it seemed that we had little leisure for conversation. At last our meditations were thus interrupted by Crites:—"You have told us how our faculties are to be improved by cultivation—how the power of attention may be weakened by neglect and strengthened by exercise—how great things may be accomplished by the bold use of the imagination, restrained at the same time within its just limits by the reason and the judgment—how much we may individually do to make or mar ourselves; and far be it from me to deny what you have said on these subjects. Still I am constantly and forcibly reminded of the great extent to which we are dependent on things external to ourselves, over which we have no control. Cooped up in my chambers during a London fog, with a headache produced by breathing a mixture of smoke and moisture, I am quite a different being from what I feel myself to be on an occasion like the present. In the one case, exertion is a painful effort;

my mind works slowly; I sit down to my task with no willing spirit. But here, breathing the pure air, with a cheerful scene around me, my thoughts flow with ease, and the exercise of my faculties, so far from being a trial, is in itself a source of content and happiness.

EUBULUS. In what you have now said you have only given us another instance of a fact as to the reality of which we are all agreed, namely, that the state of the mind, whether as regards the moral feelings or the intellect, is to a very great extent subjected to the influence of physical causes. But allow me to ask you this question. When you emerge from your chambers, under the oppression which you have described, and enter the Court of Chancery with an important case submitted to your care, do you really find yourself less capable of paying to it the necessary attention, or that you do less justice to your client, than if the air were clear, and the sun were to shine in brightly at the windows?

CRITES. I must acknowledge that, however unwilling I may be to enter on it in the first instance, when once I have become fairly engaged in the work which I have to do, my previous state of mind makes but little difference. I am not aware that I am less ready in the use of my memory, or that my attention is less complete, or that my perceptions are less acute than the occasion requires.

ERGATES. Eubulus's question sufficiently explains what is passing in his mind, and your answer to it confirms the opinion which he has intended to express. Indeed, no one, until he has been, as it were, compelled to make the necessary effort, can be aware to how great an extent the power of self-control is within our reach. It is not much to say that one whose state of health renders him fretful and peevish in his own family, may show no signs of his irritable temper when in the society of those with whom he is less intimately acquainted. On much greater occasions than this, the well-trained mind will come forth triumphant from a contest with the physical infirmities of our nature. A barrister of my acquaintance, who afterwards rose to the highest honours of his profession, was subject to a neuralgic disease, which so affected him that it often happened, when he had to advocate an important cause, that he entered the court in a state of most intense bodily suffering. But his sense of duty was greater than his sense of pain, and the latter was almost forgotten as long as the necessity for exertion lasted. The famous Cheselden, who at the same time that he was a man of science was also the most distinguished operating surgeon of the age in which he lived, thus graphically describes the feelings with which he had to contend :—" If I have any reputation in this way, I have earned it dearly, for no one ever endured more anxiety and sickness before an operation; yet, from the time I began to operate, all uneasiness ceased. And if I have had better success than some others, I do not impute it to more knowledge, but to the happiness of a mind that was never ruffled or disconcerted, and a hand that never trembled during any operation."* The commander of

* Cheselden's Anatomy, 1740, page 333.

a merchant-vessel laboured under a frightful local disease, of which it is unnecessary for me to describe the particulars. On his voyage homeward he was overtaken by a storm, during which it required the utmost energy and skill to preserve his vessel and its crew. For two or three successive days and nights he was constantly on the deck, watching everything and directing everything, as if he had been in the most perfect health. Then the storm subsided; he was again conscious of the sufferings occasioned by his complaint, and he returned home to die. In one of our former conversations, I referred to an observation of Lord Chesterfield's, that many a battle had been lost because the general had a fit of indigestion; and I presume that this may have been true as to such a Sybarite as Vendôme is represented to have been, but I cannot believe it to be at all applicable to great officers, such as Napoleon, Nelson, or Wellington.

EUBULUS. We have entered on an important chapter in the history of human nature.

If to have such a dominion over ourselves as that which you have described be necessary for great achievements, it is not less necessary to individual happiness; and well is it for those who are compelled to exercise it by the circumstances in which they are placed. The necessity of exertion withdraws our attention from the minor, and, within certain limits, even from the greater evils to which we are liable. In having to contend with difficulties, we learn to overcome them, and thus are enabled to obtain one of the highest gratifications which life affords. Nor let us overlook the fact that the exercise of the intellect, if it be applied to a worthy purpose, is not less conducive to a healthy state of mind than that of the muscles is to a healthy state of the body; and that it is in itself a source of satisfaction and content beyond any that belongs to the indolent and the lazy. Compare those who, from the duties which belong to their situation, or from their own inherent energy of mind, are always occupied, with whom the pursuit of one object, when that object is attained, leads them to the pursuit of another, with others who, having no fixed purpose, have no better resource than that of striving from day to day, or even from hour to hour, to seek some fresh amusement for themselves; and see how different is the actual amount of happiness which they respectively enjoy. To be born to the possession of what are commonly held to be the advantages of life, is, in too many instances, a real misfortune. Small evils which cannot be avoided are magnified into great ones. The Duc de St. Simon, a hanger-on of the French Court, has, with a degree of simplicity which in these days seems marvellous, graphically expressed the anxieties, heart-burnings, and other evil passions, by which he was tormented, because his master, Louis XIV., did not accord to him on small occasions that precedence to which he thought that he was entitled. So in many instances we find a too earnest attention to those slighter bodily ailments, which, if left to take their own course, would soon correct themselves, cause as much discomfort as those who are better employed experience from actual disease. The *ennui* which is the necessary result of an over-abundance of leisure is not only painful and a mighty evil in itself, but it leads to still greater evils; the victims of it, in not a few instances, being driven to seek relief by resorting to low and degrading pleasures, while in others the circumstance of the mind preying on itself produces a permanent derangement of the general health, and even to such an extent as to shorten the duration of life. The mind and the body mutually act and re-act on each other. If a healthy condition of the body conduces to cheerfulness of mind, cheerfulness of mind is still more necessary to bodily health. In more than a single instance I have received a strange confession from one who might still be regarded as a young man, and of whom others would say that he was peculiarly blessed by fortune, that he was wearied of life, finding that there was so little of real enjoyment in it! I might mention another still more remarkable instance of a gentleman, endowed with considerable intellectual powers, of great accomplishments, and having great worldly advantages, who deliberately destroyed himself, for no better reason than that he found nothing that interested him sufficiently to make him wish to live.

CRITES. They may be, and I doubt not that they are, correct, but it must be owned that you have given us but melancholy views of human nature. If Nelson or Wellington had been brought up in the Court of Louis XIV., and exposed to the same temptations as Vendôme, they might have been as profligate and idle as Vendôme himself. The over-abundance of leisure, with all the miseries and mischiefs which follow in its train, is often a misfortune rather than a fault. It seems to me that, wherever we begin, we are always brought back to the same point, and compelled to acknowledge that we are but the creatures of circumstances, these circumstances being, up to a certain point at least, independent of anything that we ourselves can do. It is not by his own choice that one boy is born and bred among thieves, or that another is spoiled by his parents and trained to idle and selfish habits.

EUBULUS. You may carry your argument further still, and say that we did not make our own minds; that we can but use the dispositions and faculties which God has given us; that our will is influenced by motives, as much as the movements of a clock are influenced by the spring which produces them, or the pendulum by which they are regulated; and thus you may find yourself involved in the metaphysical question as to necessity and free-will. Into that question I am not disposed to enter further than to make the following observations on it. *First:* finding as I do the metaphysical argument to be entirely on one side, and my irresistible conviction to be entirely on the other, I am led to suspect that this is one of the subjects to which Ergates alluded formerly as being beyond the reach of our limited capacities. *Secondly:* that, even if we admit the doctrine of a necessity which rules our thoughts and actions to its full extent, the practical result is in no way different from what it would have been if we rejected it altogether. If I am not mistaken, it was the late Baron Alderson who on some occasion addressed a jury to the following effect, if not in these exact words: "The prisoner is said to have laboured under an uncontrollable impulse to commit the crime. The answer to which is that the law has an equally uncontrollable impulse to punish him." * We may make an allowance for the external influences which operate on men's minds; we may excuse altogether those who labour under the illusions of actual insanity; but otherwise we cannot get rid of the feeling of responsibility as regards either ourselves or others: and the most thorough-going Necessarian, when he quits the loftier regions of Metaphysics to mix in the ordinary affairs of life, thinks and reasons precisely in the same way as the most unhesitating believer in free-will.

ERGATES. In short, whatever our specu-

* Memoir of Baron Alderson, by Charles Alderson, Esq., p. 128. See additional note A.

lative opinions may be, practically we are all constrained to acknowledge that, however much our intellectual and moral character may be influenced by external causes, more depends on ourselves than on anything besides. This great truth cannot be too strongly impressed on the minds of younger persons by all those to whom the business of education is intrusted, whether it be parents, or tutors, or religious instructors. The wise man, having once learned this lesson, continues to educate himself during the whole period of his life. In doing so, he soon discovers to how great an extent his mental faculties are influenced by his bodily condition, and how necessary it is that he should regulate his habits and mode of life accordingly.

EUBULUS. I need not say that I quite agree with you in the last observation which you have made, as I have myself more than once expressed the very same opinion formerly. I might indeed find much to say on the subject, for it is one that has often occupied my mind; but the questions which arise out of it belong rather to physiology, and I do not pretend to be a physiologist.

ERGATES. Yet the study of it is not peculiar to the physiologist; he only goes shares in it with the moral philosopher. There is no one, whatever may be his condition in life, and having to exercise his wits even in the humblest way, who is not perpetually reminded that there are occasions on which his capability of doing so is affected by his bodily condition.

I probably have not much to say which may not already have occurred to yourself; and I must request of you to bear in mind that the subject has been frequently referred to by both of us on former occasions; so that as to many of the observations which I have now to offer, it is probable that they may call forth from our friend Crites the remark that I am but repeating what has been already said.

The nervous force is consumed equally in mental and in bodily exertion; and if overmuch of it be expended in one way, there must be proportionally less to be expended in another. The zealous student may be induced to obtain his knowledge at the expense of his digestion; while another, who is afflicted with an appetite for food beyond the actual requirements of his system, and thus imposes too hard a duty on his digestive organs, is rendered unfit for study.

It is too much to expect that children who have been working in a factory in the morning should profit from anything beyond a very short attendance on a school in the evening. If they do so, it must be at the expense of their bodily health, and probably not without injury to their constitution. Nor in the case of adults, with the exception of the very few whose physical powers and mental energies are much above the average, is it probable that those who have been laboriously occupied in the early part of the day will be able to accomplish much in the way of attaining knowledge and the improvement of their minds in the evening. Other things being the same, a state of perfect bodily health, in which all the animal functions are well and regularly performed, is that which is most favourable to the exercise of the mental faculties. If some persons of delicate health have been distinguished for their superior intellectual attainments, that is in great measure because they have reserved their powers for the last-mentioned purpose, and have not wasted them in other ways. You referred yesterday to instances of young men who after too severe a course of study have been for a long time rendered incapable of mental labour. Here we must suppose that the intellectual exertion has exhausted the stock of nervous force. But the same thing may happen in other ways, as the result of violent emotions, especially of the depressing passions, disappointments, anger, fear, anxiety of mind. All these operate in the same manner, by using up the nervous force, and therefore interfere with the exercise of the intellect. The man of business, whose mind has been agitated during a succession of dangerous speculations, must reckon on these being rendered still more dangerous, in consequence of his judgment becoming impaired. He too will suffer in another way from the derangement of his animal functions and the injury to his general health; and this state of things, reacting on the mind, cannot fail to aggravate the original mischief.

CRITES. Then it may be inferred from what you say, that if we suppose a person to exist whose mind is not subject to be in those states which you have designated under the name of emotions and passions, in him the purely intellectual faculties, such as reasoning, thought, and judgment, would exist in greater perfection than in others?

EUBULUS. I will take the liberty of answering for Ergates that we can suppose no such thing. As, in the animal body, if you could take away the liver or the heart, or any other of the vital organs, so essential are these to each other that there would be an end of the entire system, so would the whole mind be at an end, or at least be rendered good for nothing, if any one of the faculties or qualities, or whatever else you please to call them, of which it is composed could be abstracted from it. It is only when those to which you have just alluded exist in excess that they have the ill effect which Ergates has pointed out; otherwise they are essential to the working of the whole, by affording motives for action, and by supplying materials for and exciting the imagination. In short, such a being would be beyond the pale of human nature, belonging to a mode of existence of which we can form no conception.

ERGATES. You are quite correct in your observation. The mind may be in different conditions, and is constantly passing from one of these conditions to another; but it is always one and the same mind, and, in whatever state it may exist at the time, subject to the same influences. Thus, to take a familiar instance to which I have adverted in one of our former conversations, in an aggravated case of gout, where there is an unusual accumulation of lithic acid in the blood, the temper is peevish and fretful; fits of anger are produced without any adequate provocation, at the same time that, the capability of continued attention being impaired, the reasoning faculty and the judgment are rendered imperfect. So also, where, from the want of a due supply of food, there is an insufficient production of the nervous force, it is not in one respect, but in all respects, that the mind suffers. In the latter case the impoverished blood is deprived of those properties without which it is incapable of maintaining the functions of the nervous system; while in the former case it is not that anything is wanting, but that there is an undue proportion of one of the materials of which the blood is composed, and that to such an extent that it actually operates as a poison.

CRITES. From what you have now said, and from what you said formerly, the conclusion is that the state of mind in any one of us is very much dependent upon the state of the circulating blood.

ERGATES. Undoubtedly it cannot be otherwise, so far as the state of mind is dependent on the physical organization. If a certain dose of opium causes its peculiar visions to be presented to the mind, and if a larger dose produces sleep, the narcotic poison must have first entered into the blood. So it is with chloroform, alcohol, tobacco, the Indian hemp, and a multitude of other agents which it is needless for me to enumerate.

CRITES. But I suppose you will allow that it is only when they are admitted in excess that such agents are really deleterious. Otherwise, indeed, man, as an intellectual and moral being, must have been from the very beginning of history, and must still be, in a bad way; for there never was a time when one or more of the articles which you have enumerated were not in use, and under all forms of society, from that of extreme barbarism to that of the most highly-bred civilization.

ERGATES. I admit that it seems to be something like an instinct which has led mankind in all ages to have recourse to them; and that, even independently of the use of these things as remedies for disease, there is no one of them which may not, under certain circumstances, be actually beneficial. But a large proportion of the evils to which human nature is liable arises from the abuse of the natural instincts; and there is probably no one of these the abuse of which has been productive of greater evils than that which I have now mentioned. The most obvious example that can be adduced is in the case of alcohol. A moderate quantity of it taken into the system is productive of no harm, and may be really useful; but we all know how monstrous are the evils which arise from its being taken in excess. We are too often reminded of the degrading effects which this kind of intemperance produces, both on individuals and on society at large, for me to venture to occupy your time in expatiating on them. There are, however, two points connected with this subject on which I would make some remarks: —

First. It is not simply as a liquor producing absolute intoxication that alcohol may be injurious. One person may drink a pint of port wine or an equivalent quantity of some other liquor daily, and that through a long life, with impunity; while in the case of another, though never in a state of intoxication, the effect may be to render him dull in early life, prematurely stupid in his old age, and probably shorten his life ultimately.

Secondly. The evils arising from the use of alcohol have been fearfully aggravated by the invention of distillation. It is under the influence of gin and brandy, much more than of beer or wine, that bodily diseases arise, and it is alcohol in these forms especially that leads to acts of violence and crime.

Mutatis mutandis, what I have said as to the use of alcohol may be applied to other articles of the same class, such as opium and tobacco. The opium-taker is only negatively mischievous to society; he is dreamy and inactive, but nothing more; and it is worthy of note that the habitual use of opium does not, like that of alcohol, seem materially to shorten the duration of life. So as to tobacco. In the Polytechnic School of Paris it was found that the habitual tobacco-smokers were far below others in the competitive examinations. Tobacco-smokers, like opium-takers, become lazy and stupid, but they have not the vices of gin-drinkers. As to the effect of tobacco upon the organization generally, I am inclined to think that it is more deleterious than opium, and more productive of disease, when the use of it is carried to excess.

If we had sufficiently accurate methods of analysis for the purpose, we should probably find in many instances that insanity may be traced to some alteration in the constituent parts of the blood, or to something added to it that does not naturally belong to it. A person of my acquaintance swallowed by mistake nearly a wineglassful of tincture of quinine. The first effect of it was to produce some very disagreeable symptoms affecting the head, which however subsided in about twenty-four hours. These were followed by a very inconvenient amount of deafness, which continued for several days. For some considerable time afterwards he was troubled with another symptom, the appearance of phantoms having the form of portraits of heads and faces with old-fashioned wigs, a large number of them presenting themselves at the same time in groups. These phantoms could be made to disappear by an act of the will, and might be conjured into existence in the same manner. There was therefore no danger of their being mistaken for realities, otherwise they would have been very like the illusions of a lunatic. Of other medicinal agents which are found to be useful in the treatment of disease, it is reasonable to suppose that there are none which, if given in too large a quantity, or continued during too long a period of time, will not do harm instead of good; and I might refer to instances of a state bordering on that of insanity being the result of such an abuse of remedies, and not subsiding until they were discontinued. Facts of this kind, however, may be regarded as belonging exclusively to medical science, and I do not therefore trouble you with any further notice of them. If such facts are of any value, it is not so much because they instruct us as to any definite rules of conduct, but because they serve to illustrate a principle which it would be well for every one to observe who is desirous of turning his faculties to the best account, so that the employment of them may be as useful as possible to himself, and, I may add, to others.

EUBULUS. You have done quite right in making this last addition. Man is a gregarious animal, and as such is peculiarly situated; the gift of articulate speech bringing him into more intimate relations with others of his own species than we can suppose to be the case in the societies of inferior creatures. However selfish any one may be, these relations cannot be ignored; they come across him at every turn of his life; and if it be important that he should study his own condition with a view to what immediately concerns himself, it is not less important that he should do so with reference to his dealings with others. Ergates has, on more than one occasion, explained how in all of us the temper of the mind may be affected by certain conditions of the body, and how these again may be dependent upon our peculiar habits of life. Hence the same individual who is at one time peevish and ill-tempered, and apt to take offence, may at another time be quite the reverse. To be in what is called "good spirits" is simply the enjoyment of those agreeable feelings which arise from the different organs of the body working well together, and from the animal functions being properly performed. One result of this is a cheerful disposition; but that implies a great deal more, for, however it may be in greater matters, it leads to sympathy with others in all the smaller concerns of life. Hence we find that those who by their personal influence have become the leaders of mankind have almost invariably been cheerful persons. There is, as Ergates observed in one of our former conversations, a state of mind in which every feeling has something painful superadded to it. No one, under these circumstances, can be habitually cheerful, and it is only by a constant effort to watch over his words and actions that he can compensate for this defect. Yet, if he would do justice to himself and be useful to others, the effort must be made. The effort may be more difficult to some, less difficult to others, but still it may be made by any one who has the right use of his reason;

and although we may make a due allowance for those to whom the difficulty is the greatest, we cannot regard any sane person as altogether divested of that moral responsibility which is one of the conditions of human existence.

CRITES. Do you observe that you are now reverting to a question which you discussed in the beginning of our conversation to-day, when you remarked how "the well-trained mind will come forth triumphant from a contest with the physical infirmities of our nature"?

EUBULUS. In discussions of this kind such repetitions cannot well be avoided; there being so close a connexion between the different parts of the subject, that in treating of any one of them we constantly find ourselves on the confines of another. Indeed, one principal difficulty in the study of that science which relates to the phenomena and laws of mind may be traced to the same source. Writers class the mental faculties as if they were absolutely distinct from each other; and indeed such a classification is necessary to the conduct of inquiries of this kind. But, in reality, as indeed Ergates has already suggested, those different conditions of the mind to which we give the name of the mental faculties, are so mixed up together, no one of them can be said ever to exist separately. For example, in a system of logic the imagination is altogether disregarded; but in practice it is quite otherwise, and even the pure mathematician would find that he could make but little progress in the advancement of his science, if he did not call in the aid of his imagination.

CRITES. Without disputing the truth of anything that you have now told us, you must excuse me for saying that it seems to me that you are both taking but a one-sided view of human nature. Man is a compound of mind and body. You have explained how he is to make the most of those faculties which belong to him as a being endowed with intelligence; but you have said nothing of those corporeal faculties which he possesses in common with other animals. But assuredly it is no mark of wisdom to regard perfection of any one of the faculties with which we are endowed with indifference.

In our anxiety for the improvement of the intellect, we should avoid the error of underrating the aspirations of those who strive to excel in those things which belong to the body rather than the mind. Now, little as I may excel in these ways myself, I hold that to be capable of enduring fatigue, of performing feats of strength, to be a perfect horseman, the surest marksman,—these, and such as these, seem to me to be worthy objects of pursuit. I should be well pleased if, like the πόδας ὠκὺς Achilles, I could contend with horses in a race; or if, like Ulysses, I could bend the bow that was useless in other hands; or if I could emulate Leander and Byron in swimming across the Hellespont. Although it is chiefly to the exercise of the higher functions of the mind that we are indebted for that more perfect civilization which now exists among us, it cannot be denied that, if mankind had trusted to these alone, there would have been no civilization at all. If it be true that man is inferior to many animals in all the applications of muscular force, in the strength of his limbs and of his jaws, and that his physical powers would have availed him but little in his contests with storms, and floods, and ferocious beasts, if they had not been under the direction of a superior intelligence, it is not less true that the latter, by itself, would have afforded him but a sorry protection against the various causes of destruction by which he was surrounded. Nor indeed is the case very much altered when the highest degree of civilization has been attained. Knowledge and intelligence would never of themselves have been sufficient to produce those marvellous results which are everywhere manifested around us. It is by the intellect of one class directing the physical powers of another that we have been put into communication with the most distant regions of the earth. Without such a combination there would have been no navigation, no intercourse of nations, no railways; nor would that mighty engine which supplies the very limited population of our own island with a greater amount of mechanical force than belongs to the 330 millions of the Chinese empire, have ever been called into existence, or controlled and managed even if it had been so. Then, even as regards individuals, we must not overlook the fact that there are a multitude of occasions on which the combination of intellectual with physical power is indispensable to great achievements. Taking all these things into consideration, is it not plain that the cultivation of the physical ought to be a subject of attention as much as that of the intellectual faculties in the early part of life?

EUBULUS. The answer to your question is, that for the one purpose it is quite sufficient to trust to man's natural instincts, while it is not sufficient to trust to them for the other. A boy left to himself, without the help of a tutor, would run, and leap, and climb, and play cricket, and use his muscles in all sorts of ways; but it would be a very rare occurrence for him, of his own accord, to learn to read or write. The legislature, therefore, have done wisely in directing their attention to the latter object, and taking no account of the former.

ERGATES. Any direct interference with the

training of the corporeal faculties, even if it were possible, would indeed be ridiculous. Much, however, may be done, and much indeed has been already done, by means of the sanitary measures now in progress for maintaining the masses of the population in that state of general health on which the capability of physical exertion so much depends. At the same time it is plain that it is impossible to devise any sanitary measures which would do all that is required. It is not to be expected that the artisans in crowded cities, living in close habitations, and to a great extent indulging in intemperate and thriftless habits, can enjoy the robust health and the physical powers of a rural population. There needs no other proof of this fact than the difference in the actual mortality of the two classes. Unfortunately, it is shown by the returns under the late census, that while there is a great increase going on in the population of the larger towns, the population of the rural districts is diminished rather than otherwise. I own that I cannot contemplate such facts as these without some apprehensions as to the future. There may not be any great difference observable in the course of a single generation; but is there not danger that, after a few more generations have passed away, the race will degenerate, and that the mass of the population will no longer be distinguished for those powers of physical exertion, and that unflinching determination to overcome difficulties, which have hitherto contributed so much to the power and welfare of our country?

THE FOURTH DIALOGUE.

Human Happiness.—Promoted by Civilization.—Theories of Happiness.—Happiness affected not less by Physical than by Moral Causes.—Enjoyment of Life experienced by Travellers sustained by simple Food and living in the open Air.—Trampers and Gipsies.—Some Doubts on the Subject.—Feelings of Melancholy without any evident Cause, how to be explained.—Ill-consequences of *Ennui*.—Prison Discipline and Separate Confinement.—Influence of Anxiety of Mind in deranging the Health and producing actual Organic Disease.—General Conclusions.—We must not expect too much of Life.—The Fable told by Socrates in the "Phædo."—Good and Evil necessary Parts of the same System.—Origin of Evil.—Relative Proportion of Good and Evil.—Condition of the Lower Animals in this Respect.

Crites availed himself of an early opportunity of renewing the conversation in the following manner:—"I have been listening to your lecture on the management of the intellectual faculties, and I have no doubt that the healthy exercise of those faculties is in itself a source of enjoyment; while at the same time the opposite effect is produced by whatever tends to their degradation. Still it is plain to me that neither in the one way nor the other is the sum of human happiness materially affected. I know many who have had no advantages as to education, or, if they had, did not avail themselves of them, whose thoughts have been directed to the most ordinary pursuits, and who nevertheless seem to be really happier than some of my wisest and most highly-informed friends. But is not to be happy the first object which we have in view, mixed up in some way or another with every thought and action of our lives,—'our being's end and aim, for which we bear to live, and dare to die'? Without denying the importance of the subjects which we have lately discussed, it seems to me that it would answer a better purpose if we were to inquire how we should proceed so that we should pass through our pilgrimage here with the smallest amount of painful feelings; how we may be cheerful and contented, defying the evil and taking advantage of the good which lies in the path which we are to tread."

EUBULUS. I am not aware that those whose education and habits lead them to exercise the higher faculties of the mind have less actual enjoyment of existence than others. That society generally profits by the labours of those who in any way enlarge the boundaries of knowledge is plain enough, for these are the real civilizers of mankind. It might be sufficient for me to refer to what Ergates said on this subject on a former occasion; but it may be further observed, that as the advancement of knowledge leads to the advancement of civilization, so it also tends to the prolongation of the average duration of human life. And from this last-mentioned circumstance we must presume that the result is, on the whole, a greater amount of happiness, as, with some rare exceptions, whatever tends to shorten life is productive of either physical pain or moral suffering.

But, before we proceed further, it may be as well for us to come to a more precise understanding as to what we are talking about; and I would ask, what is the exact meaning which you attach to the word "happiness"?

CRITES. Indeed, I attach to it none but the most common-place and vulgar signification. I consider him to have the greatest amount of happiness who has the largest proportion of agreeable, and the smallest proportion of painful feelings, be they either physical or moral.

EUBULUS. What you call the most common-place is, I apprehend, the most philosophical sense in which the word can be used. We must measure happiness, not by what lookers-on would say of us, but by what we feel ourselves. A man may succeed in all his undertakings, may be beloved by his family and friends, and enjoy the respect and esteem of the world; but you would scarcely call him happy if he laboured under a perpetual toothache. Do you remember the account which Pythagoras, then in the shape of a cock, is supposed to give to the shoemaker, in one of Lucian's "Dialogues," of his position when at another epoch of his transmigration he appeared on earth as a powerful sovereign? He describes how he was living in luxury; how he was worshipped almost as if he had been a god; how, as he was carried through the streets, the people assembled on the house-tops, admiring him and envying his condition; yet he adds that he could not help comparing himself to those large and gorgeous statues, the works of Phidias or Praxiteles, which are outwardly ivory and gold, but which, on the inspection of the interior, are found to be full of rats and other vermin.

CRITES. Your first illustration is quite to the purpose; but you might well have spared the second. I trust that the definition which I have given is sufficient to show that I labour under no such vulgar delusion as that which you mean to expose — against which we are warned not only by the best religious and moral writers, but even by the story-books which we have read as children.

EUBULUS. Do not suppose that I would pay you so ill a compliment as to attribute to you the belief that there is any intimate connexion between the possession of great worldly advantages and happiness. That is as it may happen. They are good for some, especially for those who may look upon them as the result of their own exertions—they may be actually bad for others; while, for the most part, they are neither the one nor the other. My object was merely to bring us to the consideration of the manner in which the subject has been treated by others.

> "Semita certè
> Tranquillæ per virtutem patet unica vitæ."

This is true, but it is not the whole truth; for we see every day that the most virtuous person may have his tranquillity of mind destroyed by circumstances which are not under his control.

At an early period of my life I was set to read a discourse on happiness by the learned author of "Hermes;" but it was as a lesson, and I had not then sufficient knowledge of human nature or of the affairs of life to form a correct judgment as to what it might be worth. An accident led me to read it again lately; and I did so with that interest with which we are apt to return to the studies of our youth. After a long, and, I must add, rather a tedious argument, conducted, as the author believed, according to the Socratic method, the conclusion arrived at amounts to this, that the way to be happy is to be always under the influence of virtuous motives. But here also I say that this is true, but that it is not the whole truth. Practically we see that the most upright and virtuous intentions are not always rewarded by happiness in proportion, and that either moral or physical causes may operate so as to make a man miserable in spite of them. They may, and will, afford support under all circumstances, and especially in the case of those who feel that they may look with confidence to a compensation for what they may suffer here in a future and brighter state of existence; but they give no absolute exemption from the common lot of human beings.

CRITES. All of which has been told us over and over again; and which no one, who sees what goes on in the world, can venture to dispute. But you may go further than this. Do we not daily meet with instances of those for whose moral qualities we have not the smallest respect — selfish people, who live only for themselves, for the gratification of their own passions, without regard to the feelings and claims of others — who seem to have their full share of such happiness as this world can afford to any of us?

EUBULUS. Undoubtedly it is so to a certain extent, especially during the season of youth and vigorous health, while a rapid succession of events keeps the mind in a state of continued excitement, and affords no leisure for reflection. But I have lived long enough to watch the course of some such persons, and am led to believe that even in this world the day of retribution rarely fails to come at last. I have seen them, as they advanced in years, fall into a state of melancholy, amounting to hypochondriasis, for which even the most firm religious convictions afforded but an inadequate relief. A philosophical friend of mine has suggested that remorse is the destined punishment in a future state of existence. Be that as it may, I am satisfied that many, who do not own it, even to their nearest friends, are the victims of remorse even here on earth. Obvious examples of it in one of its forms are almost constantly presented to us in the daily journals, in the notices furnished by the Chancellor of the Exchequer of sums of money sent to him anonymously for "unpaid taxes." Is there any one, even of the best among us, who does not look back with regret at some errors which he has committed at a former, and perhaps distant, period of life?

ERGATES. The subject with which you began this discussion may be viewed under two different aspects, the moral and the physical. It is chiefly under the former of these that it has been viewed by the theologians and moralists who have professed to instruct us as to the surest means of obtaining happiness; but it deserves fully as much to be viewed under the other aspect also. We approached the consideration of it in our conversation yesterday, when I explained that the common expression of being "in good spirits" means neither more nor less than this, that they are those agreeable feelings which are the result of the different bodily organs acting harmoniously together, and of their various functions being well and regularly performed. The condition of which I speak may be regarded as the most perfect state of animal existence, and I doubt whether there is anything in human life that affords to the individual a greater amount than this does of actual enjoyment. It might not, indeed, suit your ambition; but you may be consoled by the reflection that it is not altogether incompatible with the highest cultivation of the intellect. Therefore it is not beneath the dignity of the greatest philosophers to entertain the question how this object can be best attained.

CRITES. That question being equally important to us all, philosophers or otherwise, we shall be very glad if you will tell us how to answer it.

ERGATES. The subject has been treated of, in one way or another, by a multitude of medical writers, who tell you how to eat and drink and sleep, and everything else. But I do not much advise you to read their books, lest you might be perplexed by the discrepancy of the opinions which they contain. Thus I have in my mind at present three treatises on diet, in each of which there is a list of proscribed articles of food. But these lists are different, and if you were to adopt them all, you would find very little left to eat. Some very simple rules indeed are all that can be suggested, and each individual must apply them as well as he can to himself. A reasonable indulgence, without the abuse, of the animal instincts; a life spent in a wholesome atmosphere, and as much as possible in the open air; with a due amount of muscular exercise. Really there is little more to say.

The agricultural labourer is tempted, by the prospect of higher wages, to migrate to a manufacturing town: he might well have been content with his former lot. In the one case he breathes an untainted air; the wheaten bread which forms the staple of his food is easy of digestion and sufficiently nutritious; and, even if he were inclined to it, his slender finances do not admit of much indulgence in the luxuries of spirituous or fermented liquors: while, in the other case, he is not only obliged to breathe the air of a crowded city, but probably of an ill-ventilated factory; being also too often tempted by his larger wages, and the society in which he lives, to indulge in sensualities which are mischievous alike to the body and the mind. Which is the happier condition of the two? The reports of the Registrar-General supply an answer to the question. The average duration of human life in the agricultural districts is beyond that of the great cities; and, for reasons which Eubulus has already given us, I do not know that we can have any better measure of the relative amount of happiness in any two classes than the rate of mortality affords. Travellers in foreign countries far removed from civilization, exposed to the vicissitudes of the seasons, often with no roof to cover them at night, and even with a precarious supply of food, describe this mode of life as having in itself a peculiar charm, which may fairly be attributed to the robust health which they enjoy under these circumstances, living as they do in the open air, and being debarred as they are from mischievous indulgences.

EUBULUS. That may be in part the right explanation of the satisfaction which it is said that such a wild life affords. But I suspect there is something more than this. There is the novelty of being suddenly relieved from the restraints belonging to civilized society, of which we are scarcely conscious while they exist, but which cannot fail to be sufficiently manifest when they are removed. I do not suppose that there are many, bred up in the midst of civilization, who would long continue to prefer so great a change, though there may be some who would—as in the instance of a friend of mine, the late Mr. Salt, who at two different periods had lived among the Abyssinians, and afterwards filled the office of our Consul-General in Egypt. Mr. Salt was a highly educated person, accustomed to the society of intelligent men in London; and yet he has repeatedly declared to me that he found so much happiness in Abyssinia, that, if it had not been for the separation from his friends, he would never have returned to his own country.

CRITES. In confirmation of the remarks which you have just made, I may mention that I know an instance in which a benevolent lady made acquaintance with a girl whom she found sweeping the street, and procured for her a situation as a domestic servant, with every comfort which such a situation could afford. The girl behaved very well; but she could not bear the change, and was very soon at her old employment in the streets again. I know another instance in which a similar experiment was made with a young person of the other sex, and with the same result. I have often been struck with the appearance of the gipsies and other trampers, who are found pitching their tents on commons and in by-lanes, and who, I must say, seem happy enough. The case of the gipsies is very much in point; they have been for some centuries roaming through the most civilized countries in Europe, and yet have never been persuaded to part with the freedom which their wild life affords, in exchange for the advantages of the civilization by which they are surrounded. But do not facts, such as those to which we have just now adverted, tend to confirm the opinion which some have held, that there may be on the whole a greater amount of enjoyment of life in an uncivilized than in a civilized community, and that those whom we contemptuously call savages are, in this respect, really better off than ourselves?

ERGATES. I put no faith in this speculation. The difference between a civilized and an uncivilized community is in the benefits arising from the larger amount of knowledge belonging to the former, as compared with that which belongs to the latter. The restrictions of savage life are at least as great as those which belong to civilization, at the same time that they are of a more painful and onerous kind. You cannot read of the exploits of the kings of Dahomey and Ashantee, or the persecutions in the way of slave-hunting and accusations of sorcery among the races of Africa, as recorded by Dr. Livingstone and

M. du Chaillu, without being satisfied on this point. At the same time, independently of all this, there is, from other causes, a much greater uncertainty as to life, arising from a less regular supply of food and the ravages of disease; so that, in these respects, the trampers and gipsies of this country are a great deal better off than the negroes. The ill-treatment of women among barbarous nations would be in itself a sufficient answer to your question. Abyssinia is much more civilized than the central parts of Africa; yet I suspect that, independently of the separation from his friends, Eubulus's friend, Mr. Salt, would not have been very well contented with his lot, if circumstances had compelled him to live there during the remainder of his life.

EUBULUS. If anything were required to show how impossible it is, in discussions of this kind, to separate the influence of physical and that of moral causes from each other, the course which our conversation has now taken would be sufficient for that purpose; for, insensibly, from the consideration of the former we have passed on to the consideration of the latter.

But now allow me to ask you, as a physiologist, how you would explain a matter which has often attracted my attention, and which I have not been able to explain myself. On some occasions I have laboured under depression of spirits, having what I may call an abstract feeling of melancholy, there being no external cause to which it can be attributed, and it being at the same time, as far as I can judge, not connected with any derangement of any one of the animal functions. Several of my friends, with whom I have conversed on these subjects, have expressed to me that they have been at times similarly affected, some of them being much more liable to be so than others.

ERGATES. I will mention to you a circumstance which I recollect to have happened to myself when I was a boy, and which seems to me to throw some light on the subject. My brothers and I had undertaken a journey, to visit a relation who was staying at the sea-side waiting to embark for India. It was rather a long journey, and it occupied us two days on horseback. I had never before had an opportunity of seeing the sea, and I had looked forward to the visit with great expectation of the pleasure which it would afford me. I was, however, disappointed so far as this, that for the first two or three days I was actually unhappy, from a feeling of melancholy which I could not account for, and which I could not get rid of. Now, from observations which I have since made, I am satisfied that the real explanation was as follows:—I was not a very strong boy, and the journey had made too great a demand on my physical powers. As a general rule, whenever and in whatever way the physical powers are much exhausted, and there is an insufficient production of the nervous force, although you cannot say that any particular organ is in fault, the individual is liable to that condition of the mind which you have described. An inadequate supply of food will have the same effect. Some of my friends have complained of depression of spirits when first they awake in the morning, which is not relieved till after breakfast, and which probably arises from the long interval which has elapsed since the dinner of the preceding day without nourishment. M. du Chaillu describes a most painful state of the nervous system which he observed among the negroes in Africa, the result of a too long abstinence from animal food. The vegetable productions which form the sustenance of these poor people do not contain all the ingredients which the human system requires, and animal food is necessary to supply the deficiency. It is true that the peasantry of England, who can obtain but very little of animal food, do not suffer in this manner; but they have wheaten bread, which answers the same purpose. A want of the proper quantity of sleep operates in the same manner, as every one must have learned from his own experience. So it is with some medicinal agents, when administered in too large a quantity or during too long a period of time—iodide of potassium and colchicum, for example. When the spirits have been artificially raised by means of spirituous or fermented liquors, the exhaustion of the nervous force causes them to be depressed afterwards. From this state of depression a further supply of alcohol affords a temporary relief, and thus we perceive how the habit of dram-drinking is generated. It is the same with the smoking of tobacco. The excitement produced by the cigar is followed by a feeling of discomfort, which another cigar relieves; and thus the occasional is converted into the habitual smoker. Opium-takers are in the same predicament. An acquaintance of mine, who was subject to this unfortunate habit, said to me, "I cannot describe to you the feeling of intense melancholy which sometimes comes over me, without my being able to give the smallest reason for it." For its relief he had again recourse to opium, and thus the bad habit was kept up and strengthened.

The slaveholders of Cuba, who, by the amount of labour which they exact from them, shorten the lives of their unfortunate negroes, have this further sin to answer for, that such gradual exhaustion of the physical powers cannot fail to be accompanied by an unhappy state of mind. A more considerate and merciful legislature has interfered in the case of children employed in the factories of our own country, who might otherwise to a certain extent have shared the fate of the slaves of the Spaniards.

CRITES. I can in some degree confirm from my own personal experience what you have said as to the effect of over-fatigue of either body or mind on the condition of the latter. But is it not also true that some amount of employment is absolutely necessary to our comfort, and that there is no much greater source of misery than the *ennui* which arises from the entire absence of occupation?

EUBULUS. You may remember that I offered some observations on this subject in one of our former conversations. Nothing can be much more distressing than that state of mind in which the thoughts are not directed to any special object, constantly shifting from one to another, and finding nothing to rest upon. It lays the foundation not only of mental but also of bodily disease; and hence it is that instances are not rare of individuals who after a very active life retire, as they suppose, to be happy, but without having provided a suitable occupation for themselves, and who do not survive the change for more than two or three years. I read an account in one of the public journals of a literary man who, being a state prisoner, was condemned by a despotic government to solitary confinement, without being allowed the use of books or pen or paper. I hope, for the sake of humanity, that the statement was untrue; otherwise I cannot imagine an instance of more barbarous cruelty. And here I may take the opportunity of observing that I had myself, at one period of my life, considerable experience as to the effects of what has been called separate imprisonment of convicts in this country. In the prisons under the immediate control of the Government, the convicts are kept constantly employed, never communicating with each other, but attending the school and chapel, taking exercise out of doors, but passing the greater part of their time alone in their cells, being employed, however, in some kind of useful labour. Where this system is carefully conducted, there is really no material suffering either of the body or mind. The greatest harm that happened to the latter was, that some of the convicts, when first set at liberty, were affected with hysterical symptoms, which soon subsided, and did not prevent them from being useful labourers in the colonies afterwards. Still, without the precautions which I have mentioned, it is difficult to say what mischief might not have happened, both mental and bodily; and this fact ought never to be lost sight of by those who endeavour to carry out the same system in other prisons.

There is no doubt that there is nothing really more necessary to the enjoyment of life than constant occupation of the mind.

ERGATES. You have referred to instances of bodily disease being the result of that unhappy state of mind, to express which we are compelled to employ the French term of *ennui*, for want of an equally appropriate epithet in English. Of course it is only when this state of mind is in excess, and continued during a long period of time, that such evil result follows. But here we find ourselves on the threshold of another inquiry of great importance, but too extensive and too difficult for us to enter fairly on it at present. I may, however, briefly remark, first, that there is too much reason to believe that long-continued anxiety of mind not unfrequently lays the foundation of actual organic disease, which, proceeding sometimes slowly and sometimes rapidly, destroys life ultimately; and secondly, that in a smaller way we have almost a daily experience of the influence which the condition of the mind has on the general health. The sudden apprehension of some great misfortune will almost immediately interfere with the process of healthy digestion. Those who, impelled by a too earnest desire to become suddenly rich, are engaged in a series of dangerous speculations, are never really in a state of perfect health; and I cannot doubt that, if we had the opportunity of tracing the history of a sufficient number of such persons to the end of their career, we should find that the duration of life is, in them, much below the average. The maxim of "*quærenda pecunia primùm est,*" which Horace describes as operating so mischievously in ancient Rome, is operating not less mischievously here; those who succeed in the race often being really as much sufferers as those who fail.

CRITES. You must excuse me if I go back to some remarks just now made by Eubulus as to the effects of the system of separate confinement of prisoners in the Government prisons; recalling to his mind at the same time some other remarks which he made last year as to the desire which we have to live in society, and which, if I recollect rightly, he described to be as much an instinct as hunger and thirst. Surely it cannot be said that any amount of occupation can really render a life happy, when the gratification of such an instinct is absolutely prohibited?

EUBULUS. I did not say that prisoners under this system are made absolutely happy; nor is it perhaps desirable that they should be so, for in that case there would be no punishment. What I said, or intended to say, was, that the ill-consequences which might otherwise have arisen may by proper management be prevented. Man is a gregarious animal, and suffers from the want of the society of those of his own race, in the same manner as other animals of the same class. Association with others is necessary, not only to his own comfort but eventually even to his existence; nor is it less necessary to the maintenance of his moral and intellectual character. It is a great mistake made by some sentimental writers, when they speak of the advantages of a retired life. Those who live much alone not only become stupid, but narrow-minded and selfish. It is by living in the world that we are rendered capable of judging what we ourselves are worth; that we are taught our own deficiencies, and at the same time what is due to others. I will take this opportunity of observing, though it may not be exactly to our present purpose, that although Walter Scott's observation, that the best part of every man's education is that which he gives himself, is quite true, nevertheless one who is wholly self-educated, however great in some respects his merit may be, labours under very great disadvantages; inasmuch as, not having had sufficient opportunity of comparing himself with others, he is in danger of placing too high an estimate on his own qualifications, and of believing that the knowledge which he possesses is peculiar to himself.

CRITES. The conclusions from all that you have now stated may, I apprehend, be expresed in a few words. Our happiness in life depends, in a considerable degree, on circumstances which are altogether beyond our own control. Domestic calamities and mental or bodily disease may affect it, in spite of anything that we can do. But even here the effect may be modified to a considerable extent, as in one instance by a pure religious faith, in another by the conviction that we do not suffer from any ill-conduct of our own. But beyond this there is much depending on ourselves, not only on our own prudence and self-command, but also on the attention which we pay to our physical condition. Now all this which you have told me is really no more than I knew very well before. I acknowledge, however, that the illustrations which your physiological knowledge has enabled you to afford have caused me to view some parts of the subject under a different aspect from that under which I should have viewed them otherwise. What I am about to say, however, may not be undeserving of your attention.

There are not a few who make the great mistake of expecting too much of life, and in whom the disappointment which necessarily follows destroys no small portion of the comfort which life would have afforded them otherwise. Eubulus made some remarks on this subject in our last conversation, and referred to the cases of young men, born to the inheritance of what are considered as great worldly advantages, as being especially liable to be misled in this manner. The mistake, however, is by no means confined to individuals of this class. We see those who in early life have been acquainted with the inconveniences of poverty, who in the efforts to escape from them have toiled in the acquirement of wealth, as if they expected that wealth alone would afford them all that they could desire to have, and who yet in the end have been grievously disappointed. One man, when this great object has been attained, perhaps far beyond his original conceptions of it, is attacked by some organic disease of which Ergates would probably say that the foundation had been laid by his former labours and anxieties, and which, after a certain amount of suffering, consigns him to the grave. In another, under similar circumstances, the mind gives way, and in the midst of wealth he suffers all the evils of the poverty from which he had been so long labouring to escape. But these are extreme cases. There are others, and those more numerous, in which those who have amassed large fortunes by their own exertions become melancholy and hypochondriacal, partly perhaps from being deprived of their usual occupation, but in a great degree also because they have learned that the object for the attainment of which they had toiled, was worth so much less than they had expected.

EUBULUS. I conclude that you refer to the examples (and these, I am afraid, are not very uncommon) of individuals who, having scarcely ever had any other object in view, have devoted themselves altogether to the acquirement and accumulation of wealth; and it must be acknowledged that you can produce none better to illustrate the proposition with which you set out. There is, as I apprehend, no pursuit really more degrading to the mind than this, nor more unsatisfactory in its results. But we are not to apply this observation to all undertakings in which men are engaged for their own advancement in the world. The statesman, who has guided his country through political difficulties, who has contributed to the promotion of education among the masses of the people, who has done his best for the improvement of the law; the engineer, whose genius has enabled him to throw a tubular bridge over the Menai strait, or to bore a tunnel through the Alps; the painter, the sculptor, the architect, who leave behind them the memorials of their art for the admiration of posterity; the man of science, who has devoted himself to the improvement of the science in which he is engaged, whatever that may be; the merchant, who opens new fields of enterprise to the industry of others; the landed proprietor, who fulfils the duty of his station; —these, and a thousand others, at the end of their career, may look back at their former labours with the satisfaction of knowing that they have contributed to the welfare of others as well as of themselves, and that they have a claim on the respect and estimation of society which the mere possession of wealth could never give them. Still I agree with you as to the importance of the mind being trained so that it may not expect too much of life; and it would be well that parents and others who are engaged in the business of education should keep this in view, and not leave the lesson to be taught only by their adventures in the world afterwards.

ERGATES. Do you remember the fable related by Socrates in the beginning of the "Phædo"? Good and Evil were always quarrelling, and Jupiter had in vain endeavoured to reconcile them with each other. At last, being provoked by finding them so intractable, he punished them by joining them together, so that wherever one was to be found, the other should be found also. Indeed, it seems to be a question whether the co-existence of good and evil, or, if you please, of pleasure and pain, is not a necessary part of the system which is established in this corner of the universe, in like manner as, in a magnet or a voltaic battery, neither the positive nor the negative pole could have an independent existence; there being, however, this difference, that of the positive and negative poles each is exactly a complement of the other, whereas, as far as we can see, good and evil stand in no such mutual relation.

CRITES. We are here on the verge of an inquiry which has perplexed the greatest philosophers, namely, that which relates to the origin of evil, and the compatibility of its existence with the benevolence of the Deity. But I suppose that Eubulus would interfere by telling us that this is one of those metaphysical speculations to which he alluded in one of our former conversations as leading to no practical result, and which really would carry us beyond the reach of the human intellect.

ERGATES. I agree with you in the opinion which I suppose that you have intended to express, that such speculations are beside our purpose. At the same time I must say there were some other suggestions offered by Eubulus in the conversation to which you have alluded, from which, if we were to pursue them further, we might learn that the solution of the problem to which you have referred is not so very difficult nor so far beyond our reach as some have imagined it to be.

Another question, however, here presents itself, which, being of a more practical nature, I am not so willing to evade. What is the proportion which, in this world of ours, good and evil, or pain and pleasure, bear to each other? Some would have us to believe that the one, others that the other, greatly predominates. What is the real truth of the matter?

EUBULUS. If different individuals give very

different answers to such an inquiry, it is because they cannot fail to be influenced partly by their peculiar temperaments, and partly by the peculiar circumstances under which they are respectively placed. There are those who endure pain from bodily disease, and that during a great part of their lives; there are others who, through a long course of years, have little or nothing to complain of in this respect; and there is an equal difference as to moral suffering, whether it be induced by circumstances not under our control, or it be the result of our own mismanagement. On the whole, however, judging from such observations as I have been able to make during an active and busy life, I cannot entertain the smallest doubt that the good very greatly predominates over the evil, and that the individual cases in which it is otherwise are but rare exceptions to the general rule. There is much of good which, from the enjoyment of it having become habitual to us, we actually overlook. The condition of bodily health in which all the animal functions are well and regularly performed is in itself a state of happiness, constituting, as Ergates informed us yesterday, what is commonly called being "in good spirits." From constant and unceasing bodily pain there can indeed be no escape; but otherwise we can scarcely say that there are any instances of either physical or moral suffering which are not to a great extent relieved at intervals by better and happier feelings.

But are we not taking a too narrow view of this question, when we limit it to what belongs to the human race? Man, in his pride, is too apt to believe that all the world is made for him; yet the earth teems with life in other forms, even in regions never trodden by man, and in corners into which he cannot penetrate, and where it has no relation whatever to him. Now it cannot be denied that the lower animals have their share of whatever evil exists in the universe. Small birds perish from cold and hunger in a severe winter; the stronger oppress the weaker; and one species prospers and multiplies by the extermination of another. Still, I cannot look on the animal creation around me without being satisfied that its habitual condition is one of actual enjoyment. In one respect the lower animals are both better and worse off than man; they seem to have little recollection of what is past, and very limited anticipations of the future. While the joys and sorrows of man depend so much on the contemplation of what may hereafter happen, they live in the present hour, the object immediately before them seeming to supersede every other consideration. That such is the fact must be sufficiently obvious to any one who possesses common powers of observation; and if I mention the following anecdote, it is simply because it affords a rather curious illustration of it. I was told it by a gentleman who was an eye-witness of the circumstance to which it relates. In a hunt the hounds had very nearly reached the fox, when a rabbit crossed his path. Apparently forgetting his own danger, the fox turned on one side to catch the rabbit, and was soon afterwards himself seized by the dogs, with the rabbit in his mouth.

THE FIFTH DIALOGUE.

Advantage to be derived from the Intercourse of different Classes of Society with each other.—Objects of Education.—Schools for the Labouring Classes.—What they may and what they may not be expected to accomplish.—Those who are over-educated may suffer intellectually as well as physically.—Exceptions to the General Rule.—Objects of the higher kind of Education.—Value of Truthfulness.—Importance of Female Education.—The Acquirement of Knowledge one Object, but not the principal Object of Education.—Mathematics and the Inductive Sciences not so well adapted to the early as to the latter part of Education.—Advantages of the Study of Language.—Greek and Latin.—Cultivation of the Imagination one of the most essential parts of Education.—The Object of Education is, not that a great deal should be learned, but that whatever is learned should be learned thoroughly.—Advantages of a Variety of Study in improving different Faculties of the Mind.—Examinations and the Competitive System—The Example of Associates more effectual than Precept.—Question as to Religious Education.

In our walks in the village there were few of the labourers whom we met with whom Eubulus did not claim acquaintance, while with some of them he entered more or less into conversation. One of us having made some remarks on the subject, he answered:—

"I do so partly on principle, believing that the isolation of the different classes, and the separation of them from each other, to such an extent as it exists in this country at the present day, is a great social evil, while I fear that it may lead to still greater evil, perhaps at no very distant period of time; partly because it is a pleasure to me to cultivate a mutual kindness of feeling between my poorer neighbours and myself; and partly also for another reason, as to which I am not quite so disinterested. We speak of the ignorance of the labouring population, especially in the rural districts, and it is quite true that they are ignorant of many things with which we are well acquainted; but, on the other hand, whoever takes the trouble of doing so will find that they have much knowledge which we do not possess. It is with them as it is with those who belong to what are called the higher classes of society. There are some who are stupid, and many who are careless, and who never much learn to observe or think for themselves. But there are still others who make their own observations on what comes under their notice, and reason upon them with perfect accuracy; and from them I have often obtained what is to me both new and curious information. I believe I am correct in stating that in the manufacturing districts most of the improvements in machinery have originated with the artisans to whom the immediate management of the machines has been intrusted; and it is difficult to say how much of the improvements of agriculture may not, in the first instance, have been derived from the casual remarks and suggestions of farm labourers. However, it is not to matters of this kind that I intended more especially to allude. There are few subjects connected with rural life as to which I have not been able to turn my conversation with my rustic neighbours to a good account, natural history being one of them.

CRITES. You speak of the knowledge and

intelligence of those who have had little advantage as to education. Am I to understand that you infer from this that education does not do so much for us as is usually supposed?

EUBULUS. Indeed I infer no such thing. Education may be, and often is, thrown away—the seed being cast on a barren soil. But education properly pursued never fails to produce a good result. Take the most intelligent of the labouring classes, and I well know that there is no one among them whose power of observation would not have been greater if he had had greater advantages as to early instruction; and under this conviction, when I first came to reside among them, I took an active part in establishing a parochial school, in which, under the immediate superintendence of a liberal-minded clergyman, the children of our village receive as much instruction as the peculiar circumstances under which they are placed enable us to afford them. Our school is a very important part of our little community, and I look forward with rather sanguine anticipation to the good which it will have produced in another generation.

CRITES. I have had little opportunity of making myself practically acquainted with these subjects; but I do not doubt that your views are correct. Although my professional employments have afforded me convincing proofs that much vice may exist in combination with knowledge, and among those who have had the greatest advantage in the way of education, yet I cannot doubt the truth of what you stated formerly, that much of the evil which exists in the world may be traced to mere ignorance. Some statistics which I have seen, showing how large a proportion of those who are convicted of crime are unable to read or write, justify this conclusion. For my own part, I cannot understand why, with the opportunities now afforded them, and with the aid of the large funds contributed by the State, and the still larger by private individuals, the education of the labouring classes should not be carried much further than it now is. The human mind being much the same in all classes, we must suppose it to be everywhere equally capable of receiving instruction; and surely some general knowledge of geography, of natural history, of the physical laws of the universe, and even of animal physiology, may be communicated to the children of a parochial school as well as to others.

EUBULUS. I am aware that in these days there are many who hold the opinion which you have now expressed. But according to my observation they prevail chiefly among those who look at these things from a distance, without having much practical acquaintance with the subject. It is, as I have already stated, most desirable that all classes should have some kind of scholastic education; and, with the means which are now available, the time certainly ought not to be far distant when those who are wholly uneducated will form a rare exception to the general rule. But the question is, what is the actual amount of education which those, whose lot it is to have to maintain themselves by their manual labour, may be expected to obtain? and I venture to say that what you suggest is much beyond that which can be generally realized. If the supply of labour were less than it is, in proportion to the demand, and the average price of labour were to be higher than it now is, the case might be different. As things now are in the rural districts, the necessities of the family are such, that the boys are generally taken away from school as soon as they are able to earn some small stipend by performing some minor duties in the fields. They rarely continue to be students for more than three or at most four years; and if they learn to read with ease, to write decently, and to perform some simple exercises in arithmetic, they have accomplished a great deal, and quite as much as those who belong to other classes of society would accomplish in the same space of time. Observe that I do not say that more than this would not be useful, but that, except under some very peculiar circumstances, more than this is impracticable; and that in this, as in other matters, we must be content to do, not what we desire, but what we can. The education of the girls, indeed, may, for the most part, be continued for a longer term; but we must recollect that of the time at their disposal a great part ought to be devoted, not to literary attainments, but to instruction in needle-work, and in what belongs to other domestic duties. Although personally I know little of what occurs in the manufacturing districts, yet I apprehend that the case of the children there cannot be very different from that of the children in the country. There they are sent to the mill at a very early age, as soon as they are able to add something to the weekly earnings of their parents. There is still a portion of the day in which they may be at school; but it must be, or ought to be, a very small portion: otherwise would it not be making too large a demand on their physical capacities? Is it to be supposed that a boy or girl who has spent the greater part of the day not only in manual labour, but in a tedious, irksome, and monotonous employment, would, as a general rule, be an apt scholar in the evening? or, if it were otherwise, will any knowledge that can thus be obtained be a compensation for the loss of that amusement and relaxation which is essential to health and happiness, and, I may add, to vigour of mind, at that early period of life? The more I consider the subject, the stronger is my conviction that as to the scholastic education of the labouring classes no more is to be expected from it than some such moderate instruction as that which I have already mentioned; it being at the same time provided that they have access to a good lending library afterwards. If anything more can be done, it must be under some peculiar circumstances, of such rare occurrence as in no way to affect the general rule.

ERGATES. There is much truth in the vulgar proverb that "all work and no play makes Jack a dull boy." I believe with you that it is only to a limited extent that the education of children can be advantageously combined with bodily labour. Even in the case of grown-up persons some intervals of leisure are necessary to keep the mind in a healthful and vigorous state. It is when it is thus relieved from the state of tension belonging to actual study, that boys and girls, as well as men and women, acquire the habit of thought and reflection, and of forming their own conclusions, independently of what they are taught, and the authority of others. In younger persons it is not the mind only that suffers from too large a demand being made on it for the purposes of study. Relaxation and cheerful occupation are essential to the proper development of the corporeal structure and faculties, and the want of them operates like an unwholesome atmosphere or defective nourishment in producing the lasting evils of indifferent health and a stunted growth, with all the secondary evils to which they lead.

CRITES. Still I am not convinced. I need only refer to the numerous instances which have been adduced of the pursuit and acquirement of knowledge under difficulties. How many are there, who, having begun life under the most disadvantageous circumstances, have at last become ornaments of the age in which they lived, as men of science, or moralists, or scholars, or even as poets! And I do not understand why, under a judicious management, the catalogue of individuals thus elevated in the scale of intellect and knowledge should not be greatly augmented.

ERGATES. I am afraid that I have not made what I intended to say sufficiently clear. I referred to what must be regarded as the general rule, and I made an exception as to what may be accomplished under peculiar circumstances; as, in those very few gifted persons in whom an earnest desire of knowledge is combined with a corresponding amount of intellectual capacity and capability of physical exertion, I take it that it will rarely happen that, in some way or another, having once made a beginning, even with the humblest kind of instruction, they will not find the means of having their aspirations gratified. But it is not while in the parochial school, but afterwards, as they approach to man's estate, when they are accustomed to think and reason for themselves, that they will seek and find the opportunities of improvement. It was as a common soldier that Cobbett so trained himself as to become not only one of the most influential political writers, but also one of the greatest masters of literary composition of his day; and it was in an equally humble station that Ferguson found leisure, while pursuing his occupations in the fields, to lay the foundation of the reputation which he afterwards acquired as a mechanical philosopher and astronomer, and that Hugh Miller, as a stonemason, grew up to be an eminent geologist.

CRITES. I agree with you that such persons must depend mainly upon themselves. But you have yourself already admitted that something may be done in the way of assisting them in the process of self-education, when you mentioned the advantages arising from the access to a lending library. The so-called Mechanics' Institutes tend to the same result, and more still might be accomplished by the establishment of museums and lectures in the larger towns. Such institutions, indeed, would have a more extended influence by increasing the appetite for knowledge in all parts of the community. Those who are born to the enjoyment of ease and affluence would ultimately profit by them not less than those who are compelled to earn their livelihood by their manual labour. It must, I fear, be acknowledged that even among the former there is a large amount of ignorance, and much that is required to be done. How many are there on whom the opportunities of a complete and long-continued education have been thrown away, who go out into the world at last with nothing better than the outward show of refinement, and, from the want of some more worthy object, betake themselves to mean and frivolous, and too frequently even to degrading and demoralizing pursuits!

ERGATES. I wish that I could dispute the correctness of your last observation. But does not this confirm the opinion which I heard expressed in a public lecture, by one of the most distinguished philosophers whom this country has produced, to the effect that there must be something wrong in the prevailing system of education among the more affluent classes, when it so frequently leads to no more satisfactory result?

EUBULUS. We must take human nature as we find it. In all classes of society there are a certain number whose minds admit of being trained only to a very limited extent; in whom there is a want of mental, as there is in others of physical power. Among those whose qualifications are of a higher order, there are some who love knowledge purely for its own sake. There are others who, not being wanting in their desire of knowledge, are also influenced by the prospect of obtaining reputation for themselves; and we must not complain of such aspirations, when we find that the consequences are so beneficial to the world at large. And here it may be observed that those who have to carve out their own fortunes for themselves possess a great advantage over those who are differently situated, inasmuch as it is with them a matter of necessity that they should make the best use of the abilities which they possess, whatever they may be.

Still, I do not mean to deny that there may

be some defects in the prevailing systems of education. It would be marvellous if it were otherwise, considering how imperfect all other human institutions are. I do not profess to point out what these defects may be, nor have I, indeed, that practical knowledge of the subject which would make me competent to do so. I may, however, venture to suggest whether, as regards the higher kind of education, too much is not attempted to be done, and whether it would not be better if the students were left to accomplish more for themselves. But even as to this there can be no general rule; there being some who are incapable of learning anything except what they are actually taught, while there are others whose natural disposition it is to teach themselves and think for themselves. Unfortunately we have no means of distinguishing beforehand these two classes from each other; and even if we could do so, there would be a difficulty in varying our mode of proceeding so as to adapt it to each individual case.

ERGATES. That may be true. And here I would refer to some remarks which you made in one of our conversations last year, as to the ill-effect produced by the great extension of the competitive system, in stimulating many to exertions beyond their powers, and in promoting the exercise of the faculty of learning at the expense of the higher qualities of observation and thought.

EUBULUS. If we are to engage in the discussion of these subjects, it will, I conceive, be better not to enter into a critical examination of the prevailing systems of education, but rather to consider generally what are the principal objects which should be kept in view, and what it is that a well-conducted education may be expected to accomplish.

To begin at the beginning. It seems to me that the first thing is that a young person should be made to understand the value of truth, not only that he should never deviate from the rule of telling the truth, but that he should on all occasions desire to learn the truth, and do this to the best of his ability, not considering whether the result will be agreeable and convenient, or otherwise. Not only is this the surest foundation of the moral virtues, but without it the exercise of the intellect, on whatever it may be employed, can lead to no satisfactory result. This, you may say, is a matter so obvious that it scarcely deserves an especial notice; and yet it is to the want of a thorough conviction as to the value of truth, and the amount of labour and caution required for its attainment, that we may trace a large proportion of the disappointments to which we are liable in the ordinary concerns of life, as well as the many erroneous notions which have been from time to time propagated, and the fact that many things which at various times have passed for knowledge in the world have proved in the end no better than a sham and an imposture.

CRITES. It is not indeed to be supposed that those who have acquired the habit of misrepresentation and exaggeration in common things can form a proper estimate of the value and importance of truth on great occasions; so that even when they have no actual inducement to deceive others, they may not be too ready to deceive themselves—drawing their conclusions from insufficient premises, being influenced by their prejudices and passions, and love of novelty, and, I may add, by their indolence. But this part of education belongs to the earliest period of life, long before the schoolmaster and college-tutor have entered on their vocations. The example of a lying nursery-maid during childhood may affect not only the moral but even the intellectual character of the individual ever afterwards.

EUBULUS. Still, if we are to inquire into the subject of education, we must, as I said before, begin at the beginning, and not lay the blame merely on the nursery-maid. The bad example of the parents themselves, and their own bad management of their children, whether it be by a system of too great indulgence or of too great severity, will often do more mischief, by inducing a lax habit as to the telling or seeking of truth, than anything that goes on in the nursery.

Nor is it only in this respect that "home-education" too frequently fails in the cultivation of those qualities which are essential to the right use of the intellect, leaving much to be undone by the individual himself, or by those to whom the special business of education is intrusted afterwards. The example of idleness and of frivolous pursuits, among those whose situation lifts them above the necessity of any regular or serious occupation, has, in too many instances, a most prejudicial influence, and places their children at a great disadvantage, as compared with those of professional men, and of others who are differently circumstanced in this respect. Those whose minds are of a higher order, it is true, overcome the difficulty; but the chances are that others will devote themselves to nothing better than the pursuits of their fathers and mothers.

CRITES. But "*quis custodiet ipsos custodes?*" You are referring to evils which are so interwoven with the intimate texture of society, that to counteract them by any human means seems to be almost a hopeless undertaking.

EUBULUS. To counteract them altogether is out of the question. Yet I am sanguine enough to believe that it may be ultimately accomplished to a considerable extent. Where the "home-education" of children is deficient, that may be chiefly attributed to the imperfect mental cultivation of the parents themselves; and you have yourself already referred to one source to which we may reasonably look for an improvement in this respect. The fact of any one class in society being more thoroughly educated and better informed cannot fail to have an influence over others. If the superior classes allow themselves to be distanced in the race, they will find ere long that they are in danger of losing the position which they occupy, with all the advantages belonging to it. Money is power, which is certainly none the less from it being combined with the *prestige* of birth and rank; but knowledge and intelligence are a greater power still, and if the two should unfortunately be placed in opposition to each other, there can be, as I apprehend, not the smallest doubt as to which of them must ultimately prevail.

ERGATES. You have certainly not overrated the importance of that early training of the mind which belongs to what you have called "home-education," affecting as it does the intellectual not less than the moral character of any one of us. And here be it observed, that under ordinary circumstances more depends on the mother than on the father; from which we may judge how necessary it is to the well-being of society that the education of the female sex should include studies of graver interest, and not be exclusively devoted, as it too often is, to the acquirement of those accomplishments which are merely graceful and ornamental.

Crites. But as you have begun the inquiry, I hope that you will pursue it further. It being granted that, by the influence of precept and of example, which is more effectual than all the precept in the world, a good foundation has been laid during the earliest period of life, what are the principal objects to be kept in view afterwards, when the business of education has been formally begun? And first, what is the kind of knowledge which is best suited to the capacities of a boy in the outset of his career as a student?

EUBULUS. Certainly, from the beginning to the end, the acquirement of knowledge is an essential part of education. But I cannot regard this as the only object, nor even as the principal object—at any rate, it is not so in the first instance. The acquirement of knowledge is the instrument by means of which the intellectual faculties are to be exercised and developed, and brought into harmony with each other. The power of attention, industry, and perseverance,—these are the qualities in which children are generally most deficient, and which stand most in need of cultivation.

CRITES. But are not these qualities to be regarded rather as natural gifts, varying in degree according to the original structure of the individual mind? Ergates will agree with me when I add that they are also dependent on the physical organization, the state of health, and other circumstances connected with the animal condition.

EUBULUS. Undoubtedly there is a great original difference in this respect. Let us suppose a given number of persons, whose situation as to external circumstances is precisely similar; we should find that some acquire habits of industry and perseverance much more readily than others. By some the power of abstraction and long-continued attention to the thing before them is attained with ease, and by others not without an almost painful effort. So it is, also, with the power of reasoning. Some minds are so constituted that they are able to take cognizance at once of the evidence on both sides of a question, discerning their relative value, and, by something like a natural instinct, coming to a right conclusion; while others, having a more limited range, blunder on, never advancing beyond a partial view of the subject, and probably wasting a vast amount of labour in groping their way among small and insignificant details, the consideration of which, by diverting their attention from things of more importance, has no other effect than that of perplexing and mystifying the judgment. But as the muscles become weak, and as the organs of sense become obtuse, if not exercised, so from the same cause do the faculties of the mind, whatever they may have been originally, run to waste if neglected; while, on the other hand, there is no one of them which may not be improved by cultivation. The exercise of the mind required for the pursuit of any kind of knowledge, whatever its ultimate value may prove to be, will in a greater or less degree answer the intended purpose. The habit of idleness may be gradually converted into that of industry and perseverance—he whose natural disposition it is to wander from one subject to another may be made to acquire the habit of attention; and the result must be to make an imperfect memory more capacious and retentive.

Crites. When you say that the pursuit of any kind of knowledge will answer the intended purpose, am I to understand that all kinds are in this respect alike, and that a good education may be obtained equally by means of any one of them?

EUBULUS. Certainly not. First, it is desirable that whatever knowledge is acquired should be such as may, in some way or another, be turned to a good account, and made the foundation of a higher knowledge, afterwards. Then different studies require the exercise of different mental faculties. Mathematics, more especially geometry, and even common arithmetic, strengthen the power of attention, and therefore are peculiarly useful to those who are naturally deficient in this respect, while the higher mathematics are absolutely necessary to those who cultivate some branches of natural philosophy, as astronomy and mechanics. Further, mathematics being a deductive science, in which, a general principle being assumed, it is afterwards applied to particular cases, it renders us better qualified to deal with other sciences of the same class, such as jurisprudence and moral philosophy. Observe that I use the term "moral philosophy" in its strict and literal sense, not applying it, as it has been applied by Dugald Stewart, to the science of mental phenomena generally.

But as questions in mathematics have nothing to do with degrees of probability*, the conclusion arrived at being either true beyond all possibility of doubt, or there being no conclusion at all, so the study of mathematics does not materially help us in those other departments of knowledge in which every question has two sides, and in which we have to compare the facts on one side with those on the other, and determine on which side the evidence predominates. It is the faculty of readily and accurately calculating probabilities which distinguishes what is commonly called a man of sound judgment, whether it be in the common affairs of life, in politics, in the investigation of history, or in the practice of professions; and for the strengthening of this faculty we are not to look to geometry or algebra, while great advantage may arise from the prosecution of some other sciences, such as natural history, chemistry, geology, or animal physiology. For this reason I apprehend that the introduction

* See additional note B.

of some one or more of these inductive sciences into the curriculum of education, which is already to a certain extent taking place, cannot fail to be productive of good, at the same time that it will answer another purpose, by supplying a store of knowledge which may be turned to a good account at a later period of life; explaining many daily occurrences which would be inexplicable otherwise, unveiling many mysteries, and counteracting the influence of numerous deceptions and impostures, by which, even in the most civilized state of society, many individuals, from their ignorance of these subjects, are liable to be misled. Nor would it be difficult to show that such studies may administer to the personal well-being and advantage of those who prosecute them. Take, for example, the last of the sciences which I have enumerated, animal physiology: even a general acquaintance with it would enable us to know something of the causes which tend to derange the bodily health, and to regulate our course so as to avoid their operation; at the same time helping us to the acquirement of that self-knowledge of which we have spoken formerly, and as to the importance of which I believe that we were all agreed.

Crites. Not at all denying the truth of all that you have now stated, still I cannot but believe that inquiries connected with mathematics and the natural sciences belong properly to the more advanced stage of education, and that they can be of little avail unless they are preceded by other studies, which are not only necessary to the study of the sciences themselves, but which can never be so efficiently pursued as at that early period when the memory is more active and more retentive than at any later period of life. Not only is it by means of articulate speech and written language that, whatever the subject may be, we obtain the most important part of our knowledge, but we use language as the instrument of thought. Without it we should be incapable of carrying on any but the simplest processes of reasoning. The study of language, which includes of course the study of grammar, is properly regarded, in all civilized countries, as that part of education which should precede all others. Of course some particular language or languages must be selected for the purpose. Whether, in this country, we are right in the preference which we give to the ancient languages of Greece and Italy, or whether Dr. Latham is right in the observation that these might be taught in some more philosophical and convenient manner than that which is usually adopted,— these are questions as to which there may well be some difference of opinion.

EUBULUS. It was far from my intention to recommend the study of mathematics and the inductive sciences as the fittest subjects for the early part of education. I agree with you in all that you have said as to the study of language being the best and surest introduction to that of other things; and I may mention another advantage belonging to it, in addition to those which you have enumerated. The practical instruction as to the rules of grammar which a boy acquires is a good foundation for the study of the philosophy of grammar afterwards, and, if he be of an inquiring mind, will lead him to it; and this last is a branch of knowledge which, interesting and important as it is in itself, is rendered still more so by the fact of it necessarily including an analysis of the mental faculties, thus leading to the contemplation and study of the mind itself.

You have expressed a doubt as to the advantage of selecting the ancient rather than the modern languages for the early part of the educational system of the present day. You may remember that on a former occasion I made incidentally some remarks on this subject. The study of these languages, which we can know only from books, requires more thought, more attention, more exercise of memory, than that of our own language, or the kindred languages of modern Europe. The boy who sets seriously to work to make himself master of Greek and Latin acquires a knowledge of grammar which he may easily apply to the language which he speaks himself. The tree may be known by its fruits. As a general rule, are not the best writers in the English language to be found among those who have been conversant with the Greek and Roman classics?

But it is not on these accounts alone that I should lament to see the day in which these studies were neglected. Can there be any compensation for losing the knowledge of Greek and Roman literature? Has it not been the foundation of the highest literature of these later times? Does it not provide for us a standard of taste, by a perpetual recurrence to which we preserve a purity of taste among ourselves? Is there any better exercise for the imagination, as we advance in life, than that afforded us by an acquaintance with the classical writers, the poets, the historians, the moralists of antiquity? Is there anything that can tend more than this to the cultivation and expansion of this great, this transcendent faculty of the human mind?

CRITES. You have, on other occasions, expressed yourself in somewhat similar terms as to the importance of the imagination. But does it not occur to you that this faculty, which you dignify with the name of transcendent, is often no better than an incumbrance, the exercise of it leading to all sorts of errors and mistakes? It really seems to me that if in the matter of education we concern ourselves at all about it, it should be rather to limit it, and repress its exuberance, than to foster and exalt it. Is it not those having a too lively imagination that, defying the rules of logic, become Mormonites and Ranters, and attracted by all sorts of visionary speculations, from the well-meant Utopia of Owen of Lanark, down to the quackeries of socialism and table-rapping? In the study of mathematics, the interference of the imagination is, as a matter of course, rejected altogether; while in the inductive sciences, as Bacon has shown us, our business is to collect facts, classify them, and draw our conclusions from them, without allowing either the one or the other to be distorted by it.

EUBULUS. Allow me to state the opposite side of the account. My remarks have been intended to refer to the imagination existing in combination with accuracy of observation and a sound judgment. The plodding man, who has great power of attention to the thing before him, but who, if he has any but a feeble imagination, rejects the use of it, may learn, as it were by rote, what others have taught; but he will be neither an inventor nor discoverer, and will really contribute nothing to the advancement of knowledge. There is an abundance of individuals who have some one faculty more than usually developed; but the really great intellects, which form the ornament and the glory of the age to which they belong, are those in which the different faculties exist in a just proportion, so that they may limit and control, and at the same time help each other. Imperfect as we all are, it would be alike vain and presumptuous to look for such perfection in this respect as our day-dreams might suggest; but it is only by those in whom there is some approach towards it that great things in any way are really accomplished.

Now there is no one faculty which is so constantly exercised as the imagination. If you could look into the inmost recesses of their minds, you would find that a large proportion of mankind live as much in the imagination as in the realities of life. It is so not only with the ardent youth who builds castles in the air, and conceives himself to be the leader of armies, who aspires

> "To scatter plenty through a smiling land,
> And read his history in a nation's eyes,"

but it is so with many of the most sober-minded and matter-of-fact individuals among us. As we walk in the streets of London, there is nothing that we see in the shop-windows, nor in the persons whom we meet, nor in the carriages which rattle by us, that is not suggestive of something else, of something that we do not actually see or hear, diverging into trains of thought and speculations having perhaps only a distant relation to the objects which are around us. The mind of him who sits before the fire, apparently idle, may be occupied with trifles, or it may be wandering over the visible universe, or soaring into higher regions still; but the imagination is always at work, ever restless, ever active either for good or for evil. Under this view of the case, you cannot, I conceive, do otherwise than agree with me in the opinion that no part of early education is more important than the discipline of the imagination, so that it should be directed to worthy objects, not discouraged or repressed, but restrained and regulated.

Observe how important a matter this is in connexion with morals. The boy who has been bred up among thieves will not be less imaginative than he whose more fortunate position has been in a more virtuous community; but how different must be the dreams and speculations of their leisure hours! Let us suppose two boys having an equally retentive memory, but that the mind of one of them is stored with the vulgar ballads which we see placarded on a blank wall in the streets, and that of the other with the most noble passages of the Greek and Latin poets, of Shakespeare and Milton, and consider how great will be the difference which these different attainments will make in their respective thoughts and conduct in all the relations of life afterwards! If the spoiled child grows up to be a selfish man, is it not because his imagination has been taught to speculate on the gratification of his own wishes and his own appetites, disregarding the just claims and rights of others? The imagination will be at work whether we will or not, nor should we wish to prevent it if we could. But the direction which it takes, while it depends partly on the original constitution of the individual mind, depends in a great degree also on the materials which it has to work with; and in this respect a great deal of good may be accomplished by the instruction and discipline of early life.

CRITES. You must not suppose that I doubt the influence which the imagination exercises over the moral character. Still, I do not see what it can have to do with those intellectual processes the object of which is to ascertain the reality of facts and to draw just conclusions from them, and which seem merely to require accuracy, patience, freedom from prejudice, and careful investigation.

EUBULUS. You may remember that some allusions were made to this subject in one of our former conversations; and what I have to say on it now can be little more than an expansion of what I intended to express on that occasion.

For the mere learning what has been done by others, little else is required than the power of attention and a good memory. These are great qualities, but without other aid they will carry you no further.

If there be a question as to a mere matter of fact, where whether it be so or not is to be determined by a comparison of the evidence on one side with that on the other, it is the imagination which helps us to explore and collect the materials, the relative value of which is to be determined by the judgment afterwards.

The experimentalist arrives at a result at which neither he nor any other has ever arrived before. Does the whole truth flash on his mind at once? Far from it. It is when he makes it the subject of meditation afterwards that his imagination brings before him the relations which it bears to his previous knowledge, enabling him to look at it on every side, and to detect sources of error which he would otherwise have overlooked, and the detection of which may modify, or even entirely alter, the views which he had been led to adopt in the first instance.

As the imagination is the essential part of the genius of the poet, presenting to him analogies and relations which are not perceived by ordinary minds, so it is the main instrument of discovery in science and of invention in the arts. To the philosopher who enters on a new field of inquiry, it furnishes those lights which illuminate his path and lead him onward in his journey,—fallacious lights indeed if he trusts implicitly to them, but far otherwise if he takes them for no more than they are worth, not supposing that they can in any degree supersede the necessity of strict observation and a hesitating and cautious judgment. Such is the history of all the great achievements in the inductive sciences; nor is it otherwise even with those sciences in which we have to deal, not with probabilities, but with absolute certainties. How many crude notions must have passed through Newton's mind before he completed the invention of fluxions! So it is with all other human pursuits, whether it be in the case of Marlborough or Wellington arranging the plan of a campaign, or of Columbus directing his course over the hitherto unexplored Atlantic Ocean, or of Watt engaged in the invention of the steam-engine. Wherever great things are accomplished, it is the imagination which begins the work, and the reason and judgment which complete it. It is the same thing on a smaller scale with the ordinary, and even with the humblest, occupations of life; and this being admitted, I revert to my original proposition, that the discipline of the imagination is an important part of early education. Here I may add, that the study of the physical sciences must be especially useful in this respect, inasmuch as they deal with matters of fact, which, being cognizable by the senses, afford us peculiar facilities of testing the accuracy of the views which the imagination has suggested, and of correcting the errors into which it might lead us by being too discursive.

CRITES. When we were speaking of the education of the labouring classes, you rather took me to task for expecting that more might be accomplished than can be accomplished in reality. But it seems to me that with respect to the higher kind of education you are yourself falling into the same error. Is it to be supposed that the mind of any young person can embrace all the variety of subjects which you have enumerated,—language, the philosophy of grammar — the last, as you say, leading to the study of the mind itself — mathematics, the natural sciences? And may I ask, are all these really necessary to the objects which education has in view? Will not such a diversity of pursuit tend to perplex rather than to help an ordinary intellect — to heap up knowledge rather than to give a healthy and vigorous action to the individual faculties?

EUBULUS. Yet you will scarcely doubt that from this variety great advantages may arise. In one kind of study one faculty is more especially cultivated, in another another, and so on. Thus every variety of mind may find its suitable occupation, at the same time that no one faculty is absolutely neglected. Then, where the attention has been limited to a single object, narrow-mindedness, and a too low estimate of everything else, are apt to be the result — faults which, if corrected at all, must be corrected by others afterwards. Nor can it be doubted that he who, after his scholastic education is completed, enters on the active duties of life with a store of general knowledge, will be much more qualified to be useful in his vocation, whatever it may be, than he whose knowledge is more limited. At the same time it would be absurd to expect that every one should be an equal proficient in every branch of study. All that I contend for is, that while each individual devotes himself more especially to those inquiries which are most adapted to his peculiar taste and peculiar talents, others should not be absolutely and entirely neglected.

In saying this, I hope that I may not be misunderstood as expecting that all young persons during the period of education should obtain a complete and profound knowledge of the subjects to which their attention has been directed, nor even of any one of them. There may be some who, from a combination of superior mental with superior physical power, form exceptions to the general rule; but such exceptions are rare. To be a great Greek scholar, or a great mathematician, or a great anything else, must for the most part be a man's own work, after what is called his education is completed. This does not imply that we should be content with the attainments of the student being merely superficial. However little he may learn, that little should be learned thoroughly, so that his mind may be trained to habits of accuracy and perseverance.

ERGATES. Some of your late observations bring us back to a subject which we in part discussed formerly. For the more intelligent students there may be, I conceive, as well too much as too little of systematic education,

Such persons, after a sufficient foundation has been laid, will do more for themselves than others can do for them. It is only by those who are thus to a considerable extent self-educated, that great things are accomplished afterwards.

The system of examinations which is now being extended from schools and colleges to professions and the public services, cannot fail to be useful if it be confined to the one object of ascertaining that the candidates have that amount of knowledge which is necessary for the position which they desire to occupy; but it will be otherwise if it be carried further than this, and especially if the principle of competition, to any considerable extent, be made an essential part of it. In a difficult and elaborate examination, those who have in the greatest perfection the capability of learning what is already known, though they may have nothing else, will have the advantage over those who observe and think for themselves; yet it is to the latter that we must attribute the higher order of talent, to whom we look for the greatest results, whether it be in the way of advancing knowledge, or in the more active pursuits and ordinary business of life.

CRITES. *Aide-toi, et le ciel t'aidera.* I doubt not that this law applies to education as it does to everything else. But there is a subject connected with these inquiries to which neither of you have adverted, but which is especially of importance as involving that principle of self-education of which you have been speaking. Example is more influential than precept. In the formation of his habits and character, at least as much depends on the society in which a young man is placed, as on the instructions of his tutors. Idleness and industry, regularity and irregularity of conduct, in other respects are alike contagious, and the advantage of the best opportunities as to education will be thrown away on one who is careless as to the choice of his companions.

EUBULUS. What you have now stated is quite true; but surely you do not mean to say that your remarks are applicable only to the earlier periods of life. Old and young, our thoughts and actions are liable to be moulded by those of our associates. A quiet man who joins a mob becomes infected with the feelings of those by whom he is surrounded, and takes a share in outrages which he would have shrunk from previously. The well-bred gentleman, who wishes to preserve his purity of taste, will do well to avoid dealing with sharpers on the race-course. I would ask Ergates if it be not true that when one young woman in the wards of a hospital is seized with paroxysms of hysteria, others do not follow her example? But here we are entering on questions which would lead us far beyond the limits of the discussion with which we set out, and on the consideration of which I am not myself prepared to enter at present.

CRITES. You have given us your views as to the requirements of education, but you have omitted one important subject. Am I to understand that religious instruction forms no part of your system, and that you consider education to have no other object than that of cultivating the intellect? If it be so, I must confess that my notions are very different from yours; nor can I conceive that to adopt such a system would be right as to those who are to be educated, or otherwise than dangerous to society at large.

EUBULUS. Nothing can be further from my intention than to recommend any course of study from which religion is to be excluded. But it is a delicate matter to treat of; and I own that I am not willing to enter into the discussion of it so far as to expose myself to attacks from dogmatic theologians. Thus much, however, I must venture to say, that the religious instruction of a young person should be of that simple kind which he can easily comprehend, teaching him that it is his duty to worship God, to love his neighbour as himself, and to cultivate that charity to others without which faith, that would move mountains, is nothing worth.

THE SIXTH DIALOGUE.

Natural Theology.—Dr. Samuel Clarke.—Derham, Paley, &c.—The Phenomena of the Universe governed by General Laws.—But the Laws which are now in operation may not have been in operation always.—Questions as to Equivocal Generation.—Beginning of Animal and Vegetable Life the Result of some Special Interference of the Creative Power.—Different Views entertained on this Subject.—Darwin, and the Origin of Species.—Probable Explanation of the Commencement of the different Varieties of the Human Race.—Facts favourable, and others unfavourable, to the Theory of Development.—Partial Views of Metaphysicians on the one hand, and of Physiologists on the other.—Dr. Prichard's Argument showing the Existence of Mind independently of Organization.—Mind of the Lower Animals.—Speculations of Bishop Butler.—Place of Man in the Scale of Creation.—Articulate Speech and Written Language.—Causes tending to the Advancement of Civilization.—Questions as to the Unity of the different Races of Mankind.

We were occupied in Eubulus's library, when Crites, who had been for some time engaged in looking over the books, apart from his friends, thus remarked:—"I see you have a long array of volumes relating to Natural Theology, beginning with Dr. Samuel Sharpe, and ending with the Bridgewater Treatises. I am aware that many of these last contain much curious information, with occasionally some interesting general views as to the course of natural phenomena; at the same time it seems to me that works of this kind are scarcely required. With regard to Dr. Samuel Sharpe's *à priori* argument, I must confess that it is to me incomprehensible; and as to the other argument, by which the existence of an intelligent Creator is inferred from the marks of design in the works of His creation, I do not see that we have really advanced much further than the Psalmist, when, some 3000 years ago, he inquired, 'He that planted the ear, shall He not hear? He that formed the eye, shall He not see?'"

EUBULUS. With respect to Dr. Samuel Sharpe's speculations, I entirely agree with you. Being no German scholar, I have perhaps no right to give an opinion as to those of the great German metaphysician, Kant;

though, from the account which I have read of them, I suspect that they are equally incomprehensible with those of Dr. Sharpe. But with regard to some other writers, such as Derham, Paley, and the authors of the Bridgewater Treatises, although they may have produced no new argument in favour of the existence of a Deity, have thev not done much to strengthen the old

Erratum.

In pages 190 and 191, *for* Dr. Sharpe *read* Dr. Clarke.

Deity has [illegible]

the phenomena of the universe? The order and regularity in the course of events is, in some instances, too obvious to have been overlooked even by the rudest of mankind. Thus, night succeeds to day; the full moon returns at stated periods; winter and summer regularly succeed each other. These, and a thousand other things, bear testimony to the fact that the phenomena of the universe are subjected to certain well-defined laws, from which, at present at least, there is no deviation. But, in a multitude of other instances, the same signs of order and regularity are not at once disclosed to our observation. Hence, in all ages, much of what goes on around us has been attributed to chance, as if that term, which is, in fact, only a confession of our ignorance, expressed something which had a real and substantial existence. Others have supposed that the natural course of events was continually interfered with in other ways. The uncivilized inhabitants of Africa, when their land is parched with drought, invoke the assistance of a rain-maker, and look for clouds and showers as the results of his incantations. The classical mythology of Greece and Italy filled the world with minor deities, who, even more than the gods of Olympus, interfered in human affairs and in the operations of nature. Ulysses is reported to have been preserved from the perils of the sea by an amulet given to him by a sea-nymph; and Horace, in compliance with the prejudices of his day, if not with his own belief, attributes the preservation of his life, when it was endangered by the falling of a tree, to the benevolence of a sylvan deity. The researches of science have opened to us wider and larger views of this universe in which we live. Eclipses of the sun and moon, which formerly were supposed to occur at random, and by which nations were alarmed, as being the portents of some impending evil, are now ascertained to be as regular in their occurrence as day and night, as the seasons and the tides. Wherever we extend our knowledge, the same signs of regularity and order are manifested; and it is plain that the minutest as well as the greatest phenomena are alike subjected to certain positive laws from which there is no deviation. Modern observations have instructed us in the law of storms; and we cannot doubt that even the smallest particle of dust raised by the wind pursues its destined course with as much certainty as the earth travels in its orbit round the sun.

CRITES. It may be so. Yet I own that it seems to me a somewhat dangerous doctrine. There have been sceptics who have believed that the laws of nature were, if I may use the expression, self-existent; and that what we now see around us is but a continuation of a system that has been going on from all eternity — thus dispensing with the notion of a great creative Intelligence altogether.

EUBULUS. Under any view of the subject, it seems to me that it would be very difficult, if not impossible, for any of us practically to separate the marks of design, and of the adaptation of means to ends, which the universe affords, but which are more especially conspicuous in the animal and vegetable kingdoms, from the notion of an intelligent Cause. There is not one of the sceptics to whom you have alluded, who would not, if he were asked the question, "What is the use of the eye?" answer, "that it is intended to be the organ of vision, as the ear is intended to be that of hearing, and as the nostrils are constructed for the purpose of smell." But what I said just now requires some further explanation. When I stated that at the present time there is no evidence of any deviation from certain established laws of nature — that if we could thoroughly know and thoroughly appreciate what those laws really are, we should be able to account for all the phenomena around us — I was far from intending to say that there has never been a period when other laws than those which are now in force were in operation, or that the time may not arrive when the present order of things will be in a similar manner superseded. Looking at the structure of the globe, and the changes in its surface which have been disclosed to the observation of geologists, we recognize the probability that there was a time when this planet of ours was no better than a huge aërolite, and in a state quite incompatible with animal or even vegetable life. The existence of living beings, then, must have had a beginning; yet we have no evidence of any law now in force which will account for this marvellous creation.

CRITES. Then am I to understand that you would reject altogether the hypothesis of equivocal generation, which supposes that under certain circumstances, even at the present time, particles of inorganic matter are brought together, and so united as to become endowed with organization and life?

EUBULUS. The question is one of great interest, and I will refer you to Ergates for an answer, knowing at the same time pretty well what that answer will be.

ERGATES. Of course Crites refers to the production of those minute creatures, known by the name of *Infusoria*, in the experiments of Walter Needham, and some others.

It is true that in these experiments certain vegetable and animal infusions, after no very long period of time, when examined by the microscope, are found to contain a multitude of minute creatures, of various forms, exhibiting signs of spontaneous motion, and multiplying their species in the usual manner. Some of these are even of a complicated structure, much beyond what might, *à priori*, be expected as the result of the first attempt of inorganic matter to enter into the realms of organic life. The subject has been so frequently discussed, that I need not trouble you with the details of the arguments which have led the most eminent naturalists to believe that these creatures are not really spontaneously engendered, but that they are derived from minute ova which are present in the air, and which, when placed under circumstances favourable to their development, burst into life: in the same way as the egg undergoes those changes which convert its contents into a bird, when placed under the influence of the animal heat of the parent. But even if this view of the matter be not correct, the case is not really altered; for, after all, the *Infusoria* are never detected except in vegetable and animal infusions, which necessarily presuppose the existence of organic life.

CRITES. Then I take it for granted that you attach no credit to the story which Virgil gives us in the Georgics, of a swarm of bees being produced spontaneously in the carcase of a dead cow?

ERGATES. Certainly I do not believe the conclusion at which Virgil had arrived; but substitute the word "bluebottle-flies" for the swarm of bees, and I can understand on what foundation the story rests. These flies deposit their eggs in the flesh of the dead animal; presently you find these eggs developed into larvæ; and these, with the peculiar rapidity which belongs to insect life, are very soon converted into flies. We cannot suppose that Virgil, who shows that he had so well and so successfully studied the natural history of bees, could himself have made such a mistake; but it might well have been made by more ignorant persons, and the great poet may be supposed to have been misled by hearsay evidence.

Before quitting the subject of this so-called equivocal generation, I would take this opportunity of adverting to a circumstance which throws considerable light upon the question. Among the minute microscopic animals to which I have adverted, there are some which, though apparently dead, preserve their vitality, so that they may be revived after a very long period of time. Thus, for example, the minute animal *Vibrio*, which constitutes the peculiar blight of corn known by the name of the Earcockles, and of which a description has been given by Mr. Baüer in one of the volumes of the "Philosophical Transactions," may be seen in the form of a dry, brown stain upon the glass, and yet, on being moistened, may be brought to life again, even so as to multiply its species, after a year's interval; and this experiment may be several times successfully repeated.

CRITES. Then, if I understand you rightly, you have arrived at these conclusions. First, that there was a time when this earth was not in a fit state for the maintenance of either animal or vegetable life. Secondly, that in its present condition there is no evidence of any law being in operation which would account for any living beings being called into existence except as the offspring of other living beings which previously existed; and that from these premises we cannot fail to arrive at this further conclusion, that the first introduction of life on earth must have been by some special act of the creative power, of which we have no experience at present.

EUBULUS. I suspect that this, really and

truly, is all we actually know on the subject. But the inquisitive mind of man, on this as on a multitude of other occasions, has attempted to overleap those boundaries by which our knowledge is limited. There are two different speculations as to the beginning of the animal creation, each of which has its advocates. The more common of these is, that at different times animals have been called into existence, such as they now are; one creation disappearing and being succeeded by another, which was to disappear in its turn. The other speculation being, that some primordial germ was originally cast upon the earth, so artistically and wonderfully constructed that it contained within itself the rudiments of every animal organ that has since become developed; and that this, by a process of gradual transformation and multiplication in the course of a long series, I will not say of years, but of ages, has caused the earth to teem as it now does with its millions of millions of inhabitants.

CRITES. If I were to choose between the two hypotheses, I must adopt the former as being consistent with the history afforded us by the Sacred Writings, and reject the latter as being inconsistent with it.

EUBULUS. I must earnestly protest against this practice of placing questions in religion and questions in science in opposition to each other, as being equally detrimental to the cause of both the one and the other. The Inquisition at Rome subjected Galileo to the torture, because he asserted that the earth moved round the sun, and not the sun round the earth. But what Galileo taught has long since been universally believed, and religious faith remains unshaken. In our own time the discoveries of geology startled the minds of some pious persons, as if these were opposed to the history of the Creation contained in the first chapter of Genesis. Yet further consideration of the subject has shown that such apprehensions were unfounded, and religious faith remains undisturbed. The truth is that it was the object of the book of Genesis to instruct us, not in physical science, but in the relations of man to his Creator. Whenever and in whatever way the human race first began to exist on earth, that was the epoch of the creation of man. The theory of the gradual development of the multitudes of living beings from one primitive germ, as first propounded by the elder Darwin, and afterwards by Lamarck and the author of the "Vestiges of the Creation," has been not unfrequently viewed with suspicion, as if it had a tendency to Atheism. Yet there can be no greater mistake. Trace back this system to its origin, and you find that it takes for granted as marvellous an act of creative power and wisdom as can possibly be conceived. In saying this, however, you must not suppose that I am advocating the hypothesis in question; for really, notwithstanding all that has been said on the subject by the learned and sagacious author of the "Origin of Species," I find so many difficulties in the way, that I am very far from being convinced of its truth; and I think there is no one who will not find a great stretch of the imagination necessary to enable him to conceive that an oyster, a butterfly, a viper, and an elephant are all derived from one common stock, and are but different forms of one original element variously developed.

ERGATES. The question is indeed a very wide one. There is abundance of evidence that the different species of animals are capable of undergoing certain transformations, so that what we now see may present appearances very different from those which the same species presented formerly. Sometimes these transformations take place gradually, in the course of many successive generations, as in the case of the despised, ill-treated, and ill-fed Bosjesman, or in that of the negroes who have been partially civilized in our West India Islands, and whose appearance is very different from that of their own race who have been taken on board the slave-ships. At other times the transformation may be sudden, arising from circumstances which we cannot explain, and which we therefore call accidental. For example, there may be an Albino boy in a family in which there had been no Albino before. Let this boy grow up to man's estate, and marry, and it is probable that one or more of his children may be Albinos like himself. But let him marry an Albino woman, and all the issue of such a marriage may be Albinos, like their parents. Suppose two such families to be placed on an island by themselves, and then to intermarry, and there would probably then be a distinct race of Albinos, as there now is of negroes. It is likely that in the earliest stages of society it was in this manner that those great distinctions of the human race which now exist had their origin. The breeders of domestic animals well understand this principle, the operation of which is nowhere more distinctly manifested than in the various races of dogs. Mr. Darwin has well illustrated the subject by his experiments on pigeons; yet he has overlooked one very essential and important fact. The transformations to which I have alluded are confined to the external form, to the limbs, to the skin and its appendages. There are bandy-legged sheep, cattle with short horns or no horns at all; dogs with long legs and slim bodies, dogs with short legs, big dogs and little dogs; Albino rabbits and dark-coloured rabbits; and so on. The Dorking fowl has an additional claw; and in one instance only, quoted by Mr. Darwin, there was an additional bone in the spine of the pigeon. But these transformations do not extend to the internal and more important vital organs, nor to the muscles and nerves, nor even to the general form of the skeleton. The negro is distinguished by his woolly hair, by his projecting jaws, the shape of his legs and heel; yet it matters not to the student of anatomy whether the subject of his dissection be a negro or an European. Those organs which are the special objects of his study, the viscera of the chest and abdomen, the brain and nerves, and, I may add, the muscles, are similar in both. The same observation applies to the various races of dogs. However different their size and external form, as to the important organs, the dissection of one tells you all that you want to know as to the rest. But still further with regard to what belongs to external form, there is great reason to believe that animals, however much this may have become altered, have a tendency, if left to themselves, to return to their original type.

The main argument on which the theory of development of which I have been speaking is founded is the resemblances and analogies, as to both structure and functions, which may be traced throughout the whole of the animal creation, and which make it appear as if the respective forms of it had been framed in a great degree according to the same pattern, partaking of a common character or type. In all of them life is maintained by the inhalation of oxygen and the conversion of it into carbonic acid, and by the assimilation with their own substance of matter which had previously formed a part of some other organic body, either vegetable or animal. Excepting those which are the very lowest in the scale, there are none which do not possess something that is analogous to muscles, brain, and nerves. The gills of fish, the air-cells of insects, correspond to the lungs of the other classes. The wings of birds represent the fore legs of quadrupeds. It is needless to multiply examples of this kind, with which every one is familiar. But even if we admit that in the course of a series of ages these and other organs may have become gradually transformed one into the other, there are instances of other organs which seem to have had no prototype, and which suddenly appear in a limited number of animals, as if by some special act of the creative power. Of this fact, the poisonous fangs, and the gland for secreting poison, of the venomous snakes, the electric battery of the torpedo and other electric fishes, and the spinning apparatus of the spider, are obvious examples. There are no structures in other animals from which we can conceive that these have derived their origin. So that even if the theory of development be true, it cannot be said to contain the whole truth; and this is sufficient to make it doubtful altogether.

Crites. Then I may conclude that you have not become a convert to this modern doctrine?

Ergates. You may conclude no more than

this: that the thing is so far beyond the limits of my experience, and that, in whatever way I look at it, I find the question so beset with difficulties, that I cannot venture to form any opinion on the subject.

EUBULUS. There is another difficulty in our way, to which you have not adverted. It is probable that, in some of the very lowest forms of animal life, the functions, such as they are, are performed merely automatically; and there is no reason to believe that these simple creatures are endowed with anything like sensation and volition, any more than vegetables. But, as we ascend in the scale of animal life, we find another principle superadded,— a principle which, even in worms and insects, is the subject of sensation and volition, and which, as we ascend still higher in the scale, we find endowed with the faculties of memory, imagination, and thought, attaining their highest degree of perfection, with the addition of a sense of moral responsibility, in the human race. Now I can conceive it possible that such a supposed primordial germ as that to which you have referred may have contained within itself the rudiments of some at least of the various organic structures to be developed afterwards; but that is quite a different thing from it being the original seat of those functions which belong to the mind and intellect. I am aware that, coordinately with an extension of the mental and intellectual faculties, there is an extension and greater complication of the nervous system, especially of that part which we call the brain. But, *à priori*, we have no more right to say that the brain makes the mind, than that the mind makes the brain. In some modern works on Physiology, I see the mind spoken of as one of the properties (or, as they now call it, forces) inherent in matter, corresponding to gravitation, electricity, magnetism, and so on; the doctrine, in fact, being, that a certain arrangement of the molecules of matter in the brain leads to the production of mind, as a certain arrangement of metals and acids in a voltaic battery leads to that of electricity. But this is a doctrine which I cannot easily accept. I cannot perceive the smallest analogy between the processes of mind and what are called the forces inherent in the molecules of matter. There is so wide a gulf between them that one can in no way be compared with the other. I have no conception of any form of matter which is not essentially and infinitely divisible; the only thing of which I have any knowledge, which is essentially indivisible, is my own mind. The materials of the body, including those which compose the brain, are in a state of constant change. The brain of to-day is not the brain of yesterday, and probably there is not a molecule left of that which belonged to it a year ago. But, amid these changes, the mind preserves its identity. The belief in the identity of my own mind is as much inherent in me, and as much a part of my constitution, as my belief in the existence of an external world; I can in no way emancipate myself from it. It is said, indeed, that we have no experience of the existence of mind or intellect, except in combination with material structures; but is it so in reality? The answer to such a question has been briefly and clearly stated by the learned author of "The Physical History of Man;" and I cannot do better than refer you to his own words:—"The whole universe displays the most striking proofs of the existence and operation of intellect, or mind, in a state separate from organization, and under conditions which preclude all reference to organization. There is, therefore, at least one being or substance of that nature which we call mind separate from organized body, not only somewhere, but everywhere."* However immeasurable the distance may be between the mightiest intellect of man and that of the Deity, it must be admitted that they belong to the same mode of existence; and I do not understand how any one who believes in the existence of a Deity can receive without hesitation the doctrine that any kind of mind can be nothing more than the result of a peculiar arrangement of the molecules of matter. But, insensibly, I have been drifting back into the consideration of subjects which we discussed last year; and I remember that

* Prichard on Nervous Diseases, Introduction.

you, Ergates, on that occasion, adduced the same argument as that which I have just quoted from Dr. Prichard.

CRITES. I own that that argument seems to me to be very well founded, and it is somewhat remarkable that it should have been so much overlooked as it has been, both by physiologists and by metaphysicians.

EUBULUS. It is less remarkable as to the former than it is as to the latter. And here I am rather glad to have the opportunity of observing that these two classes of inquirers contemplate these subjects under very different aspects. The physiologist begins with making himself acquainted with the material structure of the animal body. He then studies the functions of different organs. He finds the action of muscles regulated by the ordinary mechanical laws of matter. The circulation of the blood is subject to laws similar to those which regulate the motion of fluid under other circumstances. The changes which the blood undergoes in the lungs and in the secreting glands are altogether chemical; the eye is as much an optical instrument as the microscope; and when he comes to the brain, he is too apt to regard the mind to be simply a function of the brain, in the same manner as the secretion of bile is a function of the liver. The metaphysician begins at the other end. He studies the mind irrespectively of the corporeal system; to him it has a reality of existence beyond that which he can attribute to the material world; and Dr. Berkeley and Arthur Collier have gone so far as to give reasons for doubting the existence of the material world altogether. Neither of these, as I apprehend, pursues exactly the right course. The human mind, as it comes under our observation, is to so great an extent influenced by the condition of the body, that it cannot be the proper object of study if the latter be disregarded; while the physiologist is equally wrong in regarding the mind simply as a function of the brain, overlooking the entire want of relationship between the phenomena which the mind exhibits and those presented by the material world.

CRITES. Reverting to some of your former

observations, I must observe that they lead to rather a strange conclusion. If the mental principle in the lower animals be regarded as belonging to the same mode of existence as that in man, then we must suppose that it has the same independence of organization in the former as in the latter. But how opposite is this opinion to that which is generally entertained of the relations of man and the inferior animals to each other!

EUBULUS. But I do not see at what other conclusion we can arrive, unless we adopt the hypothesis of Des Cartes, that the lower animals are mere automatons, whose actions appear to be directed by the sense and the will, while they are merely mechanical, like those of the puppets in the Marionette Theatre. On this subject, however, I may refer you to a much higher authority than myself; the question having been raised and sufficiently discussed by a learned divine, the author of the "Analogy of Religion to the Constitution and Course of Nature."

ERGATES. The truth is, that the pride of

man has led him to overlook the facts which you have now stated, and even to regard himself as if he were the only object for which the universe is created. In acknowledging the superiority of man to all the rest of the animal creation on earth, we must at the same time acknowledge not only the possibility, but the great probability, that there are in some regions of the universe organized beings endowed with faculties as much superior to those of man, as the faculties of man are superior to those of the humblest quadruped; and such beings might with as much reason regard us as having nothing in common with themselves, as we should deny the same thing to the animals below us. If I recollect rightly, Bishop Butler, to whom Eubulus has just referred, goes so far as to believe it probable that the future life which man hopes to claim for himself will not be denied to the lower animals. But, after all, this is one of those subjects which are so entirely beyond us, that it is a pure waste of time for us to speculate upon it. It is enough for us to have some faint glimpses of the intentions of the Deity as far as we ourselves are concerned; and it is not less idle than it is presumptuous to attempt to dive further into the mysteries of His government.

EUBULUS. It would indeed be presumptuous to say that your speculation, as to the existence in some part of the universe of created beings very much superior to the human race, cannot be well founded: it being at the same time not at all so to assert that the gulf which separates man from other creatures with which we are acquainted is so great, that he may well be regarded as having a peculiar mission upon earth. Let it however be observed, that the superiority of man is to be looked for, not in what he actually is, but in what he may be made to be by cultivation. The raw material, indeed, seems to be but a poor concern. As was observed in one of our former conversations, his physical structure affords him no means either of offence or defence, compared to what belongs to many other animals. He has neither tusks, nor claws, nor rapidity of locomotion. The poor children who have been left deserted in the woods, as in the case of Peter the Wild Boy, and the Savage of Aveyron, although they have contrived, perhaps during some years, to provide a precarious subsistence for themselves, have, when discovered, exhibited very few of what may be considered as the characteristic attributes of man, and have rarely profited by instruction afterwards, so as to learn to speak; they have, indeed, generally been regarded as idiotic. The only advantage which man possesses as to his physical structure is that it is adapted to the greater powers of his intellect. His legs and feet are sufficient for locomotion, and leave his upper extremities at liberty to be employed for other purposes. The only creatures that have anything corresponding to his hands are the apes; but their hands, useful as they are for the purpose of climbing, are quite unsuited for those nice actions which belong to the human hand. If an ouran-outang were suddenly gifted with human intelligence, he would not be able to write or engrave, or make or polish a needle. In them, what we call the thumb is not a thumb in reality. Independently of its form and the position which it occupies, the muscles which belong to it are not such as would enable it to answer the purpose of a human thumb.*

But another distinction, beyond all comparison more important than that of the possession of a hand, is the faculty of articulate speech,—a faculty with which no other animal than man is endowed; for we cannot with any good reason give this appellation to the barking of a dog, or the chattering of a monkey, or to the few words which a raven or a parrot may learn to pronounce without attaching a meaning to them. The voice of other animals is limited to the modifications of sound made by the larynx; and as such it is undoubtedly useful, as affording them the means, to a certain extent, of communicating with each other. But these modifications are limited in number, and would be quite insufficient to express the multitude

* For further information on this subject the reader may be referred to the interesting observations contained in Sir Charles Bell's Bridgewater Treatise.

of ideas or thoughts, or whatever you may be pleased to call them, which belong to the mind of man. The communications of some of the smaller insects with each other by means of the contact of the *antennæ* must be a more imperfect language still; but the varieties of articulate sounds, including their simpler combinations, are almost endless, and, being so, are thus adapted to the greater requirements of the human intellect. To creatures of a smaller intellect the same faculty would be useless.

ERGATES. I cannot do otherwise than cordially assent to all that you have said on the subject of articulate speech. It may well be considered as being at the same time the most important and the noblest attribute of man. Not only does the possession of it imply a higher degree of intelligence than that which belongs to other animals, but the result of it is, that by the communication of knowledge from one to the other, and the discussion and interchange of opinions, it leads to a development of the intellectual powers far beyond that which could otherwise have taken place. Nor must we overlook the fact, that words are instruments of thought, without the aid of which it would be impossible for us to apply the reasoning powers which God has given us to any but the most simple propositions.

EUBULUS. Articulate speech is the foundation of writing and printing. Written language, like articulate speech, is at once effect and cause; the invention of it is the result of the higher intelligence which man possesses, at the same time that it leads to a greater development of that intelligence in which it has originated. I need not repeat the oft-told tale of the influence which it has exercised in extending the boundaries of knowledge; but be it observed, that, like articulate speech, it is itself a help to the operations of the mind. Thus, for example, I at this moment perfectly well remember many pieces of poetry which I learned when I was a boy; but in bringing them to my recollection it often seems to me that I have before me the book and the very page from which I first committed them to my memory. I do not say that I read them off word by word; but there is the general aspect of the page, which, by association, brings before me what otherwise might have been forgotten. To those who are deaf and dumb, writing and printing are exactly the same as articulate speech is to those who do not labour under this calamity; as others remember words which are spoken, so they remember those which are written; and I cannot doubt that they answer to them the same purpose as instruments of thought.

CRITES. Is it not reasonable to suppose that the written characters of the Chinese do not in this respect answer the same purpose as alphabetic writing, the latter exactly representing the words which are uttered, the former representing things themselves; so that the Chinese, Cochin-Chinese, and the Japanese use the same characters, although their oral languages are different? Is it not from the want of the more convenient alphabetic character that the Chinese, clever people as they undoubtedly are, have, for probably 2000 years, stopped short in the progress of civilization?

EUBULUS. Undoubtedly the influence of these two methods must be very different. In the case of alphabetic writing, the writing immediately brings to the mind the words which it was the intention of the writer to express; and, reciprocally, the words that are spoken at once suggest the written characters which represent them. It is not so as to the written language of the Chinese. The connection between the spoken and the written language is entirely arbitrary ; they do not help each other; and hence it is, that to be a perfect master of the latter is almost the labour of a life.

The arts of writing and printing may well be considered as the greatest achievements of mankind, and have contributed more than any other inventions to aid a purer and more humane religion in the advancement of civilization. Observe that I use that word in its best sense, as signifying the extension of knowledge and the humanizing our species.

But other things, many of which have been accidental in their origin, have undoubtedly contributed to the same result. How helpless an animal would man have been without the possession of fire! If the civilization of modern Europe be of a higher kind than that of ancient Greece, this may well be attributed to the progress which has of late been made in the pursuit of the physical sciences, and to the influence which these studies have exercised on other branches of learning. But what would the physical sciences have been, if it had not been for the accidental discovery of glass, improved, as it was afterwards, by human ingenuity and skill? Without it there would have been no telescopes, no astronomy; and the sailor who now fearlessly traverses the Atlantic Ocean would have hesitated to conduct his vessel far from the sight of land. What would chemistry have been, if it had not been provided with glass vessels, combining the property of transparency with the capability of resisting the action of the most powerful chemical agents? If it had not been for the discovery of the uses of iron, which must originally have been accidental, we might still have been provided with no better cutting instruments than those flint knives and hatchets which are now exciting our interest as indications of the forlorn condition of our ancestors. Much might be said on this subject, but nothing more than any one's imagination will readily suggest to him.

Crites. Another element mixes itself up with this question. Is there not a great difference in the intellectual quality of different races of mankind? Take the negro, for example, of whom we know more than of any other of those which are considered as the inferior races. The negro race occupies the greater portion of an immense continent, with all varieties of soil and climate. They are neither better nor worse than they were 2000 years ago, as rude and uncivilized as ever. Does not this seem to justify the opinion which some have held, that they should be considered as being really a different species, and the result of a separate creation?

ERGATES. I know that is an hypothesis which has been propagated in the slave states of America; I cannot, however, admit it to be well-founded. I need only refer you to some observations applicable to this subject, which I made in a former part of our conversation. The difference in structure in the negro and European races is like that which may be traced in the different varieties of dogs and sheep. The more important internal organs, those on which the maintenance of life depends, including the brain itself, are the same in both instances; in fact, the only real difference, and that a comparatively small one, is in the form of the skeleton, in the skin and its appendages. At the same time I fully admit the inferior intellectual capacity, not only of the negroes, but of many other varieties of mankind. A friend of mine was in the habit of attending the negro schools in Sierra Leone; and his report of them was, that the children, up to a certain point, learned so rapidly that, to use his own expression, it was delightful to teach them; but that they could go no further. They have, by neglect, degenerated from the higher type of human nature. It is reasonable to conclude that, if properly cared for, they would gradually improve; and you may recollect that I formerly referred to the fact of the superiority of those negroes who had been for some generations domesticated and instructed in Jamaica, over the poor creatures who are brought to the island after having been delivered from slave-ships.

EUBULUS. But here we have entered on a field of inquiry of such vast extent, that, for my own part, I must confess that I cannot undertake the exploration of it. We have noticed some sufficiently obvious causes which tend to promote, as others tend to retard, the progress of civilization. But there are many others. How much must depend on the form of government; how much on the soil and climate; on the influence of peace and war?* A long life would not be sufficient to enable

* See Additional Note C.

the most diligent inquirer to answer all the questions that might be raised; and it would be idle for us to attempt to do so in the brief space of time which we can afford for a discussion of this kind. There is only one further observation which I shall venture to make. I do not doubt the possibility of negroes, or any of the other inferior races, being capable of improvement. But, even under the most favourable circumstances, such an improvement must be very gradual; and many generations of them must have passed away before it can be expected that they should even approach the point which has been attained by the more civilized communities of the present day.

THE SEVENTH DIALOGUE.

The Pony and the thorough-bred Horse.—Hypothesis of the "Indefinite Perfectibility" of Mankind.—Objections to this Hypothesis.—Intelligence and Civilization do not stand in any exact relation to each other.—Civilization promoted by the Extension of Knowledge.—Probable Improvement of the Mental Condition of the Inferior Races of Man, in the course of Time.—Future Destiny of Man.—Speculation as to the Future History of the Animal Creation.

THE day had arrived which was to terminate our second visit to Eubulus; but an inspection of the time-table showed us that we had still some time at our disposal before it was necessary to proceed to the railway station. We had made acquaintance with a rough-looking pony, in the service of some of the junior branches of Eubulus's family, which we had sometimes met with in a neighbouring meadow, and it was in reference to this animal that Crites observed: "Does it not seem remarkable that this humble quadruped should have sprung from the same stock with those beautiful thorough-bred horses which we lately saw in your neighbour's stables? Such a transformation cannot, I suppose, have been otherwise than very gradual, the result of careful culture during many successive generations. This simple fact is in itself one of great interest; but it has a still higher interest if we apply the principle on which it rests to the probable destinies of the human race. The civilized inhabitant of modern Europe is as much superior to the Australian savage as the thorough-bred horse is to your pony. In those præhistoric times when such flint knives and hatchets were in use as have lately been brought to light by geologists, the inhabitants of this very island were probably little above the condition of the Australian aborigines. You and Ergates have told us how, in the human race as well as in animals, old instincts may be lost, and new instincts may be generated, which last are capable of being transmitted from the parents to the offspring.

How much does the civilization of modern times excel that of all former ages! Taking all these things into consideration, shall we be too sanguine in our views if we speculate on a period arriving, far distant as it may be, when the qualities of the human race will have attained a much higher degree of perfection than belongs to them at present; when the intellectual powers will be more largely developed, the moral sentiments more refined; and when many of those evils which are the result of man's imperfect nature, and by which even the best form of society is now infested, will be banished from the earth?"

EUBULUS. I must first say a few words on behalf of my pony, whose character you have not rightly estimated. It is true that he has not the elegant form, nor the ease and facility of locomotion, which belong to those thorough-bred horses to which you have alluded; but he has not less power of enduring fatigue, and he is a remarkably clever and sagacious little animal. He is on terms of great intimacy with all the members of my household, and seems to consider himself as a part of my family. Physically, he may be inferior to the thorough-bred horse; but otherwise I am inclined to believe that he has the advantage over him. These facts, as you will by-and-by perceive, have an important bearing on the question which you have raised.

The "indefinite perfectibility" of man is no new speculation. It was one result of that fermentation of men's minds which existed at the period of the French Revolution, when Robespierre, rejecting vulgar superstitions, marched in a triumphal procession as the high-priest of the Goddess of Reason;

> "when busy men
> In sober conclave met, to weave a web
> Of amity, whose living threads should stretch
> Beyond the seas, and to the farthest pole;"

and when some even went so far as to believe that the time would arrive when the term of man's sojourn upon earth might be indefinitely prolonged.* The threescore years which have

* See Additional Note D.

since elapsed have, I fear, not confirmed these expectations. That some improvement, both intellectually and morally, may take place in the course of many generations, I have already admitted. At the same time we must not lose sight of the fact that, although the mental condition of the negroes of our West Indian Islands may have been rendered somewhat superior to that of their progenitors in Africa, those of Hayti are fast relapsing into their original barbarism. Do you really believe that any people of the present day possess a greater amount of intellect than those of the little country of Attica possessed more than two thousand years ago?

CRITES. Surely you must admit that the civilization of modern Europe is of a much higher character than any which has been ever attained before; and is not this fact alone sufficient to show that my speculation may not be altogether ill-founded?

EUBULUS. You may well take it for granted that those varieties or families of mankind in whom the powers of the mind are most developed are more fitted than others to enter on the career of civilization. Still it would be a mistake to suppose that the two stand in any exact relation to each other. When New Zealand was discovered the inhabitants were but savages, little better than the poor negroes of Africa; yet, from all the accounts which we have had of them, it would appear that there is no doubt as to their greater intellectual endowments. The civilization of the inhabitants of modern Europe has gone far beyond that of the same people during the middle ages. Their minds are more highly cultivated; but there is no reason to doubt that those of their predecessors some centuries ago were equally capable of cultivation, if the same opportunities had been offered to them. I need not repeat the reference which I have already made to that marvellous people of ancient Greece. The great agent in the promotion of civilization is the advancement of knowledge; and if European civilization at the present day is of a superior kind to that of Greece or Rome 2000 years ago, it is not because there is a greater amount of intellect, but because we have the advantage of the literature, art, geometry, and moral philosophy bequeathed to us by those ancient nations, with the addition of those inquiries into the phenomena and laws of nature, included under the head of the physical sciences, which the latter had neglected. The cultivation of the physical sciences has not only enabled us to obtain nobler and grander views of the universe, but, in affording us more exact information as to the reality of things around us, has been the means of dissipating many delusions and correcting many errors. This is a subject which we have in some degree discussed formerly; and I shall at present merely call your attention to the fact, that the cultivation of the physical sciences, especially within the last two centuries, has had an important bearing on other departments of knowledge, by introducing a more precise and accurate method of research. History, moral philosophy, political economy, and the science of government have, under this influence, acquired a wholly new character, and thus in various ways has the extension of knowledge greatly contributed to improve the condition of mankind. That the intellectual capacity differs very much in the different varieties of mankind is, I suppose, sufficiently obvious; nor is this very remarkable, if we consider that it corresponds with what we observe in dogs and other animals. Experience justifies the belief that some at least of the inferior varieties of the human species—the negroes for example—are capable of a higher degree of civilization than that which they have hitherto attained; and in our last conversation it was not denied by either Ergates or myself that, in the course of a series of generations, some actual improvement might take place in those respects in which their minds are now deficient: but I can find no facts which would lead me to believe that they would, under any circumstances, rise to the level of the more intellectual varieties, or that there is any law now in operation by which they will be so far elevated as to meet your sanguine expectations of the future.

ERGATES. Nevertheless, something may be urged on the other side of the question. It must be borne in mind, that, looking into the future, there is an indefinite period of time before us, during which, by however slow degrees, in a long succession of generations great changes may be worked out. For reasons which I gave formerly, I have been led to the conclusion that the whole of the human race have sprung from the same original stock; yet how great is the difference which they present as to their intellectual capacities! How then can we venture to say that, in the revolution of ages, some new variety of man may not be produced, as superior to the European of the present day as the European is to the Australian savage?

But here another view of the subject presents itself. Whatever may be the future destiny of man, is he really so perfect that he should be regarded as the crowning-piece of the creation? We have the history of the former inhabitants of our planet, not handed down by tradition, not written in books, but recorded in indelible characters in the strata immediately below the surface of the earth. We learn from these that numerous forms of animal life existed, in ages which have long since gone by, which have now become extinct; that the first of these which were called into existence were of a simpler kind; and that by a gradual, though by no means regular progression, these have been succeeded by others of a higher and a higher order. Is man to be considered as the last of these productions? or is it not more probable that he does but stand in the middle of a long series, and that in the far distant future there may be a time when, his mission on earth having been completed, he too will be replaced by other living beings, far superior to him in all the higher qualities with which he is endowed, and holding a still more exalted place in the system of the universe? You will say that this is but a vain speculation, from which no practical good can arise, and I admit the justness of the remark. If, however, such unanswerable questions sometimes present themselves to us, it is but the result of a principle implanted in the human mind for the highest and most beneficial purposes, under the influence of which we are led on in the pursuit of knowledge, some in one direction, some in another, until we arrive at that point where knowledge terminates, and we have to substitute a more or less probable conjecture for a legitimate conclusion. Such conjectures, founded on a reasonable analogy, are not to be regarded as altogether worthless. It is for us to learn where our inquiries should end, and not to bewilder our minds by the endeavour to penetrate into regions beyond the reach of the human intellect.

It was a fine afternoon, and we walked to the railway station, accompanied by our host. As he took leave of us, he said, addressing himself especially to Crites, "I am afraid that you have had but a dull visit. You might certainly have profited more, both as to your health and spirits, if, instead of being cooped up here, you had been breathing the pure air of a moor in the Highlands. It is probable that none of us are much wiser than we were before our conversations began. Nevertheless, I am led to hope that our time has not been altogether wasted. The subjects which we have discussed have this peculiar interest — that they belong to the incidents of every-day life, and that, such as they are, they are not above the comprehension of the humblest capacity, nor beneath the notice of the loftiest intelligence."

ADDITIONAL NOTES.

NOTE A. Page 85

THE doctrine of moral insanity, as expounded by the late Dr. Prichard, has been referred to in the former part of this work. The question is one of very grave importance, as bearing on the administration of justice, and there have been not a few occasions on which the misapprehension of it has led a jury to arrive at a false conclusion. The views of Baron Alderson on the subject are so clear, and his reasoning so conclusive, that no excuse can be required for transcribing the entire passage in the charge delivered by that eminent jurist from which the brief extract in the text has been taken.

"In the first place, they must clearly understand that it was not because a man was insane that he was unpunishable; and he must say that upon this point there was generally a very grievous delusion in the minds of medical men. The only insanity which excused a man from his acts was that species of delusion which conduced to, and drove a man to commit, the act alleged against him. If, for instance, a man, being under the delusion that another man would kill him, killed that man, as he supposed, for his own protection, he would be unpunishable for such an act, because it would appear that the act was done under the delusion that he could not protect himself in any other way; and there the particular description of insanity conduced to the offence. But, on the other hand, if a man had the delusion that his head was made of glass, that was no reason why he should kill another man; and that was a wrong act, and he would be properly subjected to punishment for that act. These were the principles which ought to govern the decision of juries in such cases. They ought to have proof of a former disease of mind, a disease existing before the act was committed, and which made the person accused incapable of knowing, at the time he did the act, that it was a wrong act for him to do. This was the rule by which he should direct them to be governed. Did this unfortunate gentleman know that it was wrong to strike the Queen on the forehead? There was no doubt that he was very eccentric in his conduct, but did that eccentricity disable him from judging whether it was right or wrong to strike the Queen? Was eccentricity to excuse a man from any crime he might afterwards commit? The prisoner was proved to have been perfectly well aware of what he had done immediately afterwards; and in the interview which he had since had with one of the medical gentlemen, he admitted that he knew perfectly well what he had done, and ascribed his conduct to some momentary uncontrollable impulse. The law did not acknowledge such an impulse; if the person was aware that it was a wrong act he was about to commit, he was answerable for the consequences. A man might say that he picked a pocket from an uncontrollable impulse; and in that case the law would have an uncontrollable impulse to punish him for it."

Note B. Page 168.

The mathematical calculation of probabilities cannot indeed be properly regarded as forming an exception to the general rule which has been laid down in the text. It is true that it does not lead to any conclusion which is absolutely certain, but the result is so far indisputable that it affords the nearest approach to certainty which, with the existing amount of knowledge, the human intellect can attain.

Note C. Page 226.

However much the advancement of civilization may be influenced by the operation of moral causes, such as may be included under the heads of government, religion, and education, it must be admitted that it is in no less degree influenced by the operation of physical causes also. The results of the great inventions of modern times, such as the steam-engine, electric telegraph, and railways, are too obvious to be overlooked. But we must not therefore lose sight of the fact that a multitude of inventions with which we are now so familiar that they scarcely seem to attract our notice, were in their own day not less important than those which have been just referred to. To the primæval inhabitants of the earth, the rude cutting instruments manufactured from flints were a greater acquisition than the finest steel cutlery is to those of modern Europe. Nor was there any more important epoch in the history of man than that of the first domestication of the dog, whose faithful services enabled him better to contend with the wild animals of the forest, at the same time that they assisted him in procuring the necessary supply of game for his food. The first wheelbarrow contained within itself the principle of two-wheeled and four-wheeled carriages. But the greatest and most important invention of all was the application of fire to useful purposes: without it the ores of iron and copper which lie concealed in the earth could have been turned to no account; there could have been little or no agriculture, as the grains of wheat, barley, and rice are nearly wholly unfit for the food of man unless subjected to the action of heat. The same may be said of the tubers of the potato and the roots of other vegetables; and here we have presented to us what is perhaps one of the most difficult problems connected with human history. By what experience was it possible for our progenitors to learn the uses of fire, and how was it that they first ventured to employ so fierce and terrible an agent? It may well be a question, indeed, whether this knowledge was the result of experience at all, and whether it was not rather founded on an especial instinct implanted in them for the purpose.

Note D. Page 231.

Condorcet, Progrès de l'esprit humain, chap. x.—"La perfectibilité ou la dégénération organique des races dans les végétaux, dans les animaux, peut être regardée comme une des lois générales de la Nature.

"Cette loi s'étend à l'espèce humaine, et personne ne doutera, sans doute, que les progrès dans la médecine conservatrice, l'usage d'alimens et de logemens plus sains, une manière de vivre qui développerait les forces par l'exercice, sans les détruire par des excès ; qu'enfin, la destruction des deux causes les plus actives de dégradation, la misère et la trop grande richesse, ne doivent prolonger pour les hommes la durée de la vie commune, leur assurer une santé plus constante, une constitution plus robuste. On sent que les progrès de la médecine préservatrice, devenus plus efficaces par ceux de la raison et de l'ordre social, doivent faire disparaître à la longue les maladies transmissibles ou contagieuses, et ces maladies générales qui doivent leur origine au climat, aux alimens, à la nature des travaux. Il ne serait pas difficile de prouver que cette espérance doit s'étendre à presque toutes les autres maladies, dont il est vraisemblable que l'on saura toujours reconnaître les causes éloignées. Serait-il absurde, maintenant, de supposer que ce perfectionnement de l'espèce humaine doit être regardé comme susceptible d'un progrès indéfini, qu'il doit arriver un temps où la mort ne serait plus que l'effet ou d'accidens extraordinaires ou de la destruction de plus en plus lente des forces vitales, et qu'enfin la durée de l'intervalle moyen entre la naissance et cette destruction n'a elle-même aucun terme assignable? Sans doute, l'homme ne deviendra pas immortel ; mais la distance entre le moment où il commence à vivre et l'époque commune où naturellement, sans maladie, sans accident, il éprouve la difficulté d'être, ne peut-elle accroître sans cesse?

"Comme nous parlons ici d'un progrès susceptible

d'être représenté avec précision par des quantités numériques ou par des lignes, c'est le moment où il convient de développer les deux sens dont le mot *indéfini* est susceptible. En effet, cette durée moyenne de la vie, qui doit augmenter sans cesse, à mesure que nous enfonçons dans l'avenir, peut recevoir des accroissemens, suivant une loi telle qu'elle approche continuellement d'une étendue illimitée, sans pouvoir l'atteindre jamais; ou bien, suivant une loi telle, que cette même durée puisse acquérir, dans l'immensité des siècles, une étendue plus grande qu'une quantité déterminée quelconque, qui lui aurait été assignée pour limite. Dans ce dernier cas, les accroissemens sont réellement indéfinis dans le sens le plus absolu, puisqu'il n'existe pas de borne en deçà de laquelle ils doivent s'arrêter. Dans le premier, ils le sont encore par rapport à nous, si nous ne pouvons fixer ce terme, qu'ils ne peuvent jamais atteindre, et dont ils doivent toujours s'approcher; surtout si, connaissant seulement qu'ils ne doivent point s'arrêter, nous ignorons même dans lequel de ces deux sens le terme d'indéfini leur doit être appliqué; et tel est précisément le terme de nos connaissances actuelles sur la perfectibilité de l'espèce humaine, tel est le sens dans lequel nous pouvons l'appeler indéfinie."

A doctrine so agreeable to the fancy, so gratifying to human ambition, and enunciated by so eminent an individual, could not fail to attract a certain number of disciples, some of whom were even more sanguine than their master. The alchemists had failed, but the philosopher had discovered the true *elixir vitæ.* The views of Condorcet were indorsed by Godwin, in his essay on political justice; but in his case the dream seems not to have been of long duration, as, in a very few years after the publication of that remarkable work, he gave in his romance of St. Léon a graphic description of the discomforts, and even miseries, which might be expected to arise from a life protracted much beyond the usual period. The futility of such speculations, indeed, must be sufficiently apparent to any one who bears in mind that, even under existing circumstances, the tendency of the increase of population is to overtake that of the means of subsistence, and considers to how great an extent any considerable prolongation of the period of human life must, in the course of a few generations, multiply the number of human beings on the surface of the globe.

THE END.

CPSIA information can be obtained
at www.ICGtesting.com
Printed in the USA
LVHW080000160620
658199LV00017B/371